Time
After
Time

**A true story of how one family found victory over
suffering and death in the midst of unusual circumstances**

PASTOR DENNY CARR

WESTBOW
PRESS
A DIVISION OF THOMAS NELSON

WestBow Press books may be ordered through booksellers or by contacting:

WestBow Press
A Division of Thomas Nelson
1663 Liberty Drive
Bloomington, IN 47403
www.westbowpress.com
1-(866) 928-1240

Because of the dynamic nature of the Internet, any web addresses or links contained in this book may have changed since publication and may no longer be valid. The views expressed in this work are solely those of the author and do not necessarily reflect the views of the publisher, and the publisher hereby disclaims any responsibility for them.

Any people depicted in stock imagery provided by Thinkstock are models, and such images are being used for illustrative purposes only.

Certain stock imagery © Thinkstock.

ISBN: 978-1-4497-5695-6 (sc)
ISBN: 978-1-4497-5696-3 (e)

Library of Congress Control Number: 2012911154

Printed in the United States of America

WestBow Press rev. date: 10/24/2012

Contents

In Memory of Christine Carr

Christine was not famous in the eyes of the world. However, Chris was special to me for the simple reason that she was my first child. She was a little girl of faith and intellect. Chris never lived to see her gifts come to fruition. She died of leukemia at the age of ten and a half on March 26, 1977, at Children's Memorial Hospital in Chicago, Illinois. Chris's life has left a lasting impression on family and friends who knew her story and a loving Lord who took her home with Him.

Acknowledgments

I am most grateful to family, friends, teachers, doctors, and the people from Fox Valley Presbyterian Church who in so many ways contributed to this book.

I am particularly grateful to my wife, Jan. Her profound faith and love has inspired my journey with the Lord. Her assistance in making *Time After Time* possible has been a blessing and great encouragement to me. God has also truly blessed me with three awesome children, Connie, Diane, and David, now grown up and with their own families, serve Jesus every day.

Several friends have added input to *Time After Time*. This book would not have been complete without their efforts. A special thank-you is extended to Ken and Carol Seidel for their contributions. I am also grateful to Sandy Petrille for the initial editing. My deep appreciation is also extended to Pam Weinberg for taking the time to edit the final draft. Thanks to Ken and Nancy Hennig for providing technical expertise and support. Finally, my appreciation to Lynn Metz for contributing her artistic talents on the front cover design.

Introduction

God blessed my wife, Jan, and me with a beautiful daughter on September 2, 1966. It was truly an exciting moment in our young married lives. It felt so good to say "our first child"! Those of you who have experienced the birth of your first child probably had similar feelings. Our small third-floor apartment in Berwyn, Illinois, had a tiny new addition. Our lives changed dramatically when we brought home our daughter Christine. It was no longer only about us; it was also about her. We welcomed our new responsibility as parents with great enthusiasm and love.

Chris's medical problems began at her birth. She was born with a clubfoot, which raised major concern for her young, naïve parents. She underwent surgery when she was three months old, and both of her legs were placed in casts for several months. Needless to say, seeing our little girl in those casts at the beginning of her life created some stress in our lives.

As years passed, we moved to Saint Charles, Illinois, and added two more girls, Connie and Diane, to our household. At the age of seven Chris received a diagnosis of Acute Lymphocytic Leukemia at Children's Memorial Hospital in Chicago. We were devastated. How could this be? In an instant we went from taking for granted that we had all this time to watch Chris grow up to realizing she might not live more than six months. At that moment, our world took on a totally different meaning. Life was now so precious and so short! Suddenly, we were learning the importance of living one day at a time.

Time After Time is a true story of how one family came to rely on the Lord Jesus Christ through the daily trials of coping with a terminally ill child and through it all experienced His comfort, strength, and encouragement. It's a true story of what God can do if we are open to His heart, love, hope, peace, grace, and mercy. It's a true story of encouragement, hope, and victory for those who struggle with the illness, pain, suffering, trials, and tragedies that come with living life every day. It's a story based on Romans 8:28, which says, "And we know that in all things God works for the good of those who love Him, who have been called according to His purpose."

Perhaps you have heard the line from one of Henry Wadsworth Longfellow's poems that says "Into each life some rain must fall." Each day is not guaranteed to bring sunshine and blue skies. Unpleasant experiences filled with storm clouds and rain will come our way at some time or another. That is just the way life is.

My family and I experienced many rainy days in our daughter's journey with leukemia. With the Lord's help, we survived the many storms that surrounded her illness and death. We came through them all triumphantly because of the unlimited power, grace, and mercy of a loving God. Therefore, how could we not give praise and glory to Jesus throughout the pages of this book?

May you find the Lord's blessings, power, and strength as you read the following paraphrased words from the song "Bring the Rain." Where you have pain, may you find the Lord's peace and grace. If you have doubt and confusion, may God grant you steadfast courage to overcome. If you are tired, stressed out, and want to give up, may God give you a clear understanding and strength to press on and fight another day. If you are consumed with fear, may God fill your whole being with His unconditional love.

"Bring the Rain"
Words by: Holly Cheney
(Some lyrics paraphrased)
Numerous times I have been approached
About how can I praise You God in the midst

Of all my trials
My reaction just astounds me when You
Consider what could alter my relationship with You
Yes, my life has been transformed by Your presence
Before these storms have come my way
It never dawned on me to deny You, Lord
My protection from turbulence
Brings me in Your presence
I lift up my pleas to You
I ask for joy, I ask for peace
I ask for the opportunity to be released
I ask for happiness realizing there will be times of
Disappointment
Whatever pain comes my way I will give You glory
Then Lord let the rain pour down
I will be forever Yours in spite of the storms that
Hover over me
Because You can rise above all my hurts
You have provided me with a path
By enduring pain for Your purpose
Glory, Glory, Glory
Is the almighty God

Friends, this wonderful life-changing promise comes from God's Word. He works all things for good for those who trust in His Son Jesus Christ. There is absolutely nothing we can't conquer; we can even conquer death. God can always turn something bad into something good. This is a story of finding victory in Christ while going through many horrible experiences in the midst of a terrible tragedy. If we receive Jesus as Lord and put our undying trust in Him, we are in line with God's will, meaning we are also called to His good purpose. The chapters in this book reveal how born-again, Spirit-filled Christians can be victorious regardless of the obstacles they face on this side of heaven.

For Christmas 2009, my wife, Jan, and I received a Christmas card from longtime friends who reside in Arizona. They wrote the following: "We think of you often and remember all the fun times we had. Rock music really sends us back to memory lane when we hear those familiar golden oldies."

There is no doubt that music stirs our emotions and often takes us back in time to a nostalgic moment in our lives. For example, an old love ballad may remind you of your first love: "our song." A sad song can evoke painful moments in our lives past, present, and so on. I believe God can use even the secular to lead us to the sacred.

Throughout this book each chapter starts with a paraphrased song (a golden oldie) that has stirred a memory of how the power of the living Christ helped us through the most difficult experience a parent could ever go through: the suffering and death of a child.

The heartbreaks you might be experiencing in your life may paralyze you with fear and uncertainty about what lies ahead. However, the reality is that we can have a quiet boldness, confidence, and assurance in God's amazing love, power, and ability to rise above it all.

However, at times it seems to get uglier before it gets better. It is exactly in those moments of extreme despair that we discover that God is not simply a temporary relief. Instead, we come to the realization that He is our eternal shelter, protection, and strength in any unfortunate situation we might find ourselves in. We just need to look God's way and give Him a chance to "Taste and see that the Lord is good! Happy is the man who takes refuge in Him!" (Psalm 34:8). The pages of *Time After Time* are filled with this profound truth.

Whatever you are going through, may you find the blessings of God and victory in Christ as you read *Time After Time*.

If God's truth is rejected, then living a life of confusion can be expected.

"Lady in Red"
Words by: Chris de Burgh
(Some lyrics paraphrased)

She looked so lovely her eyes sparkling,
As she moved across the dance floor.
While we danced it was as if there was only the two of us.
I was caught up in her presence
The way she looked on that dance floor was unforgettable.
Even though we just met I fell in love
With the smile on this beautiful girl's face.
I did not want to be with anyone else but this lady in red.

CHAPTER ONE

"Lady in Red"

Background

The song "Lady in Red" although popular in the 80's, takes me back to a weekend dance on the Wisconsin State University–Whitewater campus in the fall of 1964. This was a fuzzy stage in my life. I was a loose and carefree freshman just trying to find my way. It was safe to say my major that semester was partying with my buddies. The only nondrinker in our group was Mike Murray from Hales Corners, Wisconsin. Mike was our designated driver even before that title became common several years later. For most of the guys, being able to drink beer legally even though we weren't yet twenty-one was probably the best thing outside of coeds on campus. At the time, the legal age for drinking beer in Wisconsin was eighteen.

Don't Tie Me Down

I had just come out of a relationship and had no intention of getting involved in another one. For me, it was all about being free without commitment. That was my new motto.

The dances at Whitewater were a blast, and my buddy Mike taught me the finer points of dancing. I was no John Travolta, but I got by. The bands at our dances were very good and played the latest rock songs. The most popular song on campus in the fall of '64

1

was Roy Orbison's "Pretty Woman." I couldn't count the number of times I heard that song on the radio or sung by one of the local bands.

I've Gotta Be Me

I believed this was truly a good season in my young life. I was thoroughly enjoying my social environment. My academics, however, were another story. If you were to ask me at the time, I would have told you my priorities were in the right order. Since my earlier years had been filled with a number of personal tragedies I don't want to go into here, I thought I was entitled to have some fun without major worries. I was at the right place at the right time. My close college friends came from stable homes and strong Catholic backgrounds. It didn't matter how late we were out partying on Saturday night; the guys always attended Mass the following morning. I could never really understand why. Nevertheless, deep in my heart and mind, I always respected their commitment to church.

A Victim of Deception

At this point in my life, the only thing that mattered was having a good time. I could not have cared less about my responsibility as a student. I didn't even respect the fact that I had worked hard to save money so I could attend Whitewater in the first place. In college, I looked forward to happy hour. I majored in beer and partying. The sobering truth was that I had flushed all my hard-earned money down the toilet. I ignored the very purpose for going to college and pursuing an education. I wasn't blowing Mommy's or Daddy's money, but my money! There was no doubt that at the time, I was a bit twisted and deceived. Some might say, "Hey, no big deal; many young, unmotivated students have done the same thing." However, once I became a born-again Christian, I viewed those out-of-control days quite differently.

Get Out of My Face

I was deceived by the trickery of Satan, and I didn't recognize his deception. Satan was cutting my spiritual jugular vein through temptation. He was whispering in my ear, saying, "Go have your fun; you deserve it. Besides, it's your money. What good is living life if you don't have a little harmless fun once in a while?" A person can have fun and be responsible, but having fun and acting irresponsible in the process is different.

This is the evil one's trap. In the Bible, Peter wrote, "Be self-controlled and alert. Your enemy the devil prowls around like a roaring lion looking for someone to devour" (1 Peter 5:8).

On Guard

Satan does not play favorites; he does not discriminate. All of us are his fair game. Peter issued a warning to all Christians—be on your guard, be watchful, take control, and be alert. Often, many in the faith let down their spiritual guards and give Satan an opportunity to manipulate them. *Following Jesus every day keeps the Devil at bay.* The good news is that we can overcome his attacks by being attentive, fixing our eyes on Jesus, and putting our faith and trust in Him alone.

Let's Dance

One of the fall dances held at the student center started out like any other dance my buddies and I attended that wild semester. It all changed in a heartbeat when the lady in a red dress caught my eye. When I laid my eyes on this lady in red, she really got my attention. I watched her on the dance floor. My friends urged me to go ask her for a dance. It didn't take a whole lot of convincing on their part before I approached this girl in red and asked if she wanted to dance. I will never forget her smile; her face just glowed. I must be honest; the chemistry was there right from the beginning.

Getting to Know You

For the next two hours, this woman in red was the only one I saw in that massive student center. We literally danced the night away. The song "Lady in Red" brings me back to that dance floor in 1964. It felt like just the two of us were on that dance floor, and I did not want it to be any other way. For me, falling in love was overwhelming. De Burgh's song brought me back to an earlier time and my own experience with a lady in red. It was love at first sight. I will never forget what my lady in red looked like on that special night. In my eyes, she was just amazing!

The Love Bug Strikes

That fall night changed my life forever. From that moment on, Jan and I were inseparable on campus. My relationship with her wasn't simply a physical attraction; it went much deeper. She also possessed great values and a wonderful personality. Love was in the air.

Peter wrote, "Your beauty should not come from outward adornment, such as braided hair and the wearing of gold jewelry and fine clothes. Instead, it should be that of your inner self, the unfading beauty of a gentle and quiet spirit, which is of great worth in God's sight" (1 Peter 3:3-4). Peter was saying we should not be consumed with fashion or outer appearance. Although fashion, grooming, and hygiene are important, we need to keep in mind that Peter instructed women to develop inner, Christian beauty. In verse 4, Peter stressed that true beauty comes from within a person. What attracted me to Jan went beyond appearance to her inner beauty.

Meet the Parents

During the Christmas holiday of '64, I was invited to Jan's house in Berwyn, Illinois, to meet her family. While visiting her home, Jan made my favorite pie (apple). It was the best I had ever tasted. What a bonus! Could it be she was trying to set me up? We finished out the fall semester. I did not enroll for the winter term because of money issues. Jan enrolled for the winter semester while I worked in Rockford, Illinois. I drove to Whitewater on the weekends to visit Jan and my friends. In February, Jan had to drop out of college to have her appendix removed.

Popping the Question

After Jan recovered from her surgery, she went to work in a bank and planned on returning to college in the fall. In April 1965, I did the responsible thing and asked Jan to marry me, having known her for only five months. What were we thinking? Young people, I do not recommend that you follow our lead. This scary, unexpected news made her parents very nervous. They had known me for only a short period of time, and my wanting to marry their daughter without being financially stable did not exactly make their day. I can tell you theirs was not a Mike and Carol Brady response! It took some time for them to get over the shock of thinking their daughter had lost her mind. It did not come as a surprise when they viewed me with extreme caution.

The Plan

Plans were under way for a September wedding approximately one year after Jan and I had met. The plan was for me to move to Berwyn. All I needed to do was take care of one small detail—finding a job! I began my job search almost immediately and eventually began working as an apprentice meat cutter for Jewel Food Stores in the Chicago metropolitan area. My brother-in-law, a meat cutter at the time, was instrumental in getting me the job.

Our First Home

I rented a small, third-floor, three-room apartment in Berwyn. Jan's parents were not exactly thrilled that their soon-to-be-married daughter's first home would be a tiny apartment next to the railroad tracks. I was assigned to a Jewel store in Cicero, Illinois.

Lady in Red Becomes the Lady in White

Jan and I were married at the Berwyn Presbyterian Church on a hot, stormy September 4, 1965. Our marriage did not exactly have a storybook beginning. A year later, our first child, Christine, was born on September 2, 1966. I will never forget the young girl in the red dress on the dance floor at Wisconsin State University–Whitewater.

Faithless

Jan and I pretty much left God out of the first seven years of our marriage. We had wonderful friends, but our lives did not include Jesus. Our family started to grow, but our faith did not. Social drinking played a major role in our entertainment activities. One of our highlights was to drop the kids off at their grandparents' house, drive to Whitewater, and visit friends over Labor Day weekend. Drinking dominated our holiday stay. I also spent many a Saturday night after work at a little bar in Lisle, Illinois, with some of my fellow meat cutters. However, the clock was ticking, drawing us closer to a time when our whole world would be turned upside down.

Just Moving Along

In the meantime, Jan and I enjoyed what married life had to offer. Living in Berwyn, a suburb of Chicago, took some getting used to. Moving from a rural town with roughly six hundred people to a large community like Berwyn was a culture shock for me. The fast pace of city life was initially a difficult transition for this small-town boy. We took a step up in class after two years and moved into a rented house close to our tiny apartment. At the end of my third-year apprenticeship with Jewel, we bought a home in Saint Charles, Illinois, a western suburb of Chicago. Our lives moved along, but God was still not part of the equation.

The Long Wait

By the end of my apprenticeship, my life with Jan seemed to be growing in contentment, and we had some financial security. However, we were about as far away from any commitment to God as you could possibly get. We lived in a young world and anticipated exciting things ahead. Who needed God to mess up our dreams and aspirations?

A Lifeless Faith

The apostle Paul said, "The man without the Spirit does not accept the things that come from the Spirit of God, for they are foolishness to him, and he cannot understand them, because they are spiritually discerned" (1 Corinthians 2:14). Paul was describing me; I was not saved, and my priorities were the things of this world. I sought and was content with all the goodies the world had to offer. Therefore, it was impossible for me to discern or understand the things of the Spirit. The Holy Spirit of God was a foreign concept in my eyes. The idea that God could dwell in my heart and mind was not a viable option for me. However, spiritual help and God's special revelation were on the way. *A life driven by selfish ambition leads to a critical spiritual condition.*

Jesus can lift you up when your problems are weighing you down.

"It's My Party and I'll Cry if I Want To"
Words by: Walter Gold, John Gluck Jr. and Herb Weiner
(Some lyrics paraphrased)

My boyfriend disappeared with another girl
And I couldn't understand why they were holding hands
When he was my boyfriend not hers
I was brought to tears at my own party
You would have reacted the same way if you were me.

CHAPTER TWO

"It's My Party and I'll Cry if I Want To"

Shortly after we moved to Saint Charles, I was transferred to another food store closer to our home, which made it more convenient. My goal was to work hard, with the hope of one day being promoted to the position of market assistant manager. Things were going well as far as I was concerned. I became a market assistant manager, and my family was expanding.

Our second daughter, Connie, was born May 28, 1969. The following May, our third daughter, Diane, was born May 21, 1970. My life seemed to be in order. We were living in a growing, progressive community. I had a wonderful wife, three healthy children, and a job that suited me at the time. What else did I need?

Before Christ

Paul said, "The man without the Spirit does not accept the things that come from the Spirit of God, for they are foolishness to him, and he cannot understand them, because they are Spiritually discerned. The spiritual man makes judgments about all things, but he himself is not subject to any man's judgment" (1 Corinthians 2:14-15). In verse 14 Paul was talking about non-Christians. In those days, I was not a born-again, Spirit-filled Christian. I was chasing the values and pleasures the world offered. As verse 14 suggests, I was not driven by a Spiritual wisdom that comes from having a personal relationship with Jesus Christ. In verse 15, Paul talked about the Spiritual man, the Christian who was controlled by the very Spirit of God and not the natural flesh. The Spiritual person can have insights into God's thoughts and purposes. I was not operating in any form of Spiritual wisdom that comes from having an intimate relationship with Jesus Christ. I was baptized, and believed in God in a general sense, but I certainly was not focused on real faith in those days. I was so busy following the desires of the flesh I could not have cared less about seeking to understand the thoughts of God.

On the Outside Looking In

During those early years in our marriage, we joined Fox Valley Presbyterian Church in Geneva, Illinois. Why? Because Jan had been a member of the Presbyterian denomination. I basically joined the church to please her. I went to church on special occasions or when the kids were involved in the children's programs. One could say I was a typical CE Christian, meaning I showed up at church on Christmas and Easter. When I did go, after the service was over, it was "Feet, don't fail me now"—I was out the door in a hurry! I did not want any part of those churchgoing people. Besides, I thought they were nothing more than a bunch of hypocrites.

Give Me a Break

I spent my Sunday mornings paying homage by worshipping the *Chicago Tribune* newspaper. Isn't that what hardworking men were supposed to do? I felt I had earned the right to sleep in on Sunday mornings after putting in forty-plus hours at my job. For me it was "working hard for the money" and then a much deserved rest at the end of the week. It most certainly was not about putting on my Sunday church clothes and mixing with a bunch of church people. It was all about relaxing, watching sports on TV, and visiting family. Mellowing out and resting was my priority. The idea of spending time with God was not on my "important things to do" list.

Everything Was Beautiful

The kids were growing. Chris was now in second grade; Connie and Diane were four and three respectively. Raising the kids and running the household kept Jan very busy. Everything was falling into place. Our lives seemed to be complete. I believed we were part of the average American family fabric. As those early months and years passed, I was content. As far as I was concerned, we were living the *Father Knows Best, Leave It to Beaver, Donna Reed Show* lifestyle. Life was not too complex for us; things were simple and routine. Nothing appeared to be missing or out of the ordinary in our happy little middle-class family.

Then It Happened

Jesus said, "I have told you these things, so that in Me you may have peace. In this world you will have trouble. But take heart! I have overcome the world" (John 16:33). Jesus was sharing with His disciples a basic reality of life. There will be struggles, there will be pain, there will be problems, and there will be failure along life's journey. Time was also closing in on Jesus. He was about to be arrested and crucified. Yet in the midst of it all, Jesus offered His followers and us peace and joy in the heat of battle. He promised us victory when He said, "But take heart! I have overcome the world." Little did I realize just how much Jesus' words would soon ring true in our lives. As parents we would be facing the most horrific news imaginable.

The Ride

Chris had always been a very good student. She took her school studies seriously. One day Jan received a note from Chris's teacher, saying she was having problems paying attention and had fallen asleep in class on a few occasions. Chris seemed tired and experienced frequent headaches and bruising. Jan took her to our family physician for an examination. After running a few tests, the doctor called Jan with a concerned voice. He said something was wrong and that we needed to take Chris to Children's Memorial Hospital in Chicago for further tests. Filled with fear, Jan asked if she had leukemia. He replied that he didn't know. Jan, Chris, Connie, and Diane picked me up from work.

Our drive on the expressway heading downtown to Chicago was fearful and gut wrenching. I remember as a kid having a fellow student die of leukemia. His death affected not only me but also the rest of the class. Those thoughts and memories were running through my mind. My anxiety grew with each passing mile. Chris was pale and lethargic; our unspoken fears filled the car. It was an extremely tense ride for sure. There wasn't any joking, trivia, or small talk, or admiring the magnificent skyscrapers that lined Lake Shore Drive. It was a very quiet and sobering time, filled with many questions about what to expect when we arrived at Children's Memorial Hospital. Questions filled our minds. What tests would they perform? When would we get the results? What would they reveal? Would she be hospitalized? It was the longest, most nerve-racking drive we had ever experienced.

The Arrival

We arrived at Children's Memorial Hospital late in the afternoon on April 15, 1974. Jan's parents met us at the hospital and took Connie and Diane home with them. I had to carry Chris from the parking lot to the hospital entrance. She was getting weaker with each passing hour.

From the moment we stepped foot into the hospital, we felt overwhelming support. Chris was placed in a wheelchair, and we were led to one of the third-floor evaluation rooms. The staff had already received her initial tests. Two hematologists, Dr. Lee (who would become Chris's favorite doctor) and Dr. Schwartz, entered the examining room. Both appeared very confident and self-assured, but not in a boastful way, which gave us some degree of comfort. As a result, we felt some relief and assurance in the midst of the storm of uncertainty that swelled around us. We were confident Chris was in capable hands. The professionalism of the entire staff at Children's Memorial Hospital was apparent from clerks, nurses, technicians, and doctors. They were all just amazing. We knew our daughter was at the right place.

Our Big Concern

Dr. Lee examined Chris and began to ask us some probing questions about her general physical condition. We answered each question while our eyes darted from the doctor to our pale, listless daughter. During this whole ordeal, our little girl looked exhausted and seemed to lack energy. It wasn't natural to see a seven-year-old in such a state. I just knew something was wrong, terribly wrong! They drew several vials of blood and ran a series of clinical tests. Then we had to wait for the results.

The Shocking News

I cannot recall exactly how long we had to wait there in the examining room, but I can say without a doubt that it felt like forever. We talked about a variety of things, trying to keep our minds off of what might be. Our inner suspicions were that she had leukemia, but of course we hoped we were wrong and tried to think positive thoughts and convey them to Chris. The unfamiliar sounds of a busy hospital kept drawing us back to the reality of why we were there. Finally, Dr.

Lee called us into the conference room and told us straight out that our daughter had Acute Lymphocytic Leukemia. He assured us that Chris's chances were very good and that chemotherapy treatments could put her in remission. We asked how long she would be in remission if the treatments were successful, but Dr. Lee could not give us a definite answer.

Total Devastation

We were totally devastated. One sentence changed our lives forever. "Your daughter has leukemia." I was so devastated that I found it difficult to organize my thoughts and feelings. My greatest fear had become a reality. We had been given a death sentence. In an instant we went from taking for granted that our daughter would grow up, go to college, get married, and have children, to suddenly knowing that every moment with her was precious. I could not waste one day, one moment, one hug, one kiss, or one I-love-you.

Flowing Tears

Chris was in the hospital for a week after her diagnosis and went into remission within a month. This was a painful time for us. As Chris's father, I felt helpless because I couldn't fix her. I couldn't protect her from this deadly disease. I was at a party, a horrible party I did not want to attend. In the coming weeks there were nights when I would enter Chris's bedroom while she was asleep, sit in her rocking chair, and just weep. I cried a lot in those days. I'm sure that if you had a child, you would have cried too if it happened to you. My tears kept flowing, because my heart was broken. I couldn't fix my daughter. I couldn't make her feel better. I couldn't make her normal again. I couldn't give her a long, happy life. Yes, like the song goes, it was my party and I was crying because I wanted to.

How Can I Get It?

As my struggles of trying to deal with Chris's disease continued, I noticed a calm in Jan that bordered on eerie. I fired questions at her because she was experiencing a newfound peace and strength when I was overwhelmed with torment over our tragic news. She seemed to have found a quiet understanding in the midst of the storm, whereas I found nothing but helplessness. I was hopelessly cracking up. I desperately wanted what Jan had, but I did not know how to get it.

Transformation

As I grilled Jan, she gently shared how a friend from church, Sandy Petrille, had led her into the saving knowledge of Jesus Christ as her personal Lord and Savior. Jan was reading the Bible every day, and I witnessed firsthand how she received comfort from the power of the Word. *If you want to be in Jesus' presence, then you must trust in His essence.* Jan placed her trust in Jesus as Lord and Savior. As a result, the very Spirit of God transformed her life and her thinking, by redirecting her mind and heart to spiritual things. "Do not conform any longer to the pattern of this world, but be transformed by the renewing of our mind. Then you will be able to test and approve what God's will is—His good, pleasing and perfect will" (Romans 12:2).

Believing the Lord

Jesus calmed the storm.

> One day Jesus said to His disciples, "Let's go over to the other side of the lake." So they got into a boat and set out. As they sailed, He fell asleep. A squall came down on the lake, so that the boat was being swamped, and they were in great

danger. The disciples went and woke Him, saying, "Master, Master we're going to drown!" He got up and rebuked the wind and the raging waters; the storm subsided, and all was calm. "Where is your faith?" He asked His disciples. In fear and amazement they asked one another, "Who is this? He commands even the winds and the water, and they obey Him." (Luke 8:22–25)

A storm blew in while Jesus' disciples were fretting and anxious. Like the disciples, when storms come our way, we often panic, not knowing what to do. Well, my response was like Jesus' disciples in that boat. A great storm had swept into my life, and I panicked because my faith was nonexistent. However, when this terrific storm came upon Jan, instead of trying to control her circumstance, she placed a deep trust in her Lord and found calmness.

A journey to the cross is well worth the cost.

"All I Need Is a Miracle"
Words by: Neil Christopher and Mike Rutherford
(Some lyrics paraphrased)

I am in need of a miracle.
I am in need of a miracle.
When I catch you
I will love you forever.
I am in need of a miracle

CHAPTER THREE

"All I Need Is a Miracle"

Terror Strikes

Three months into Jan's conversion experience, I was still blown away by her ever-increasing faith. My inquiring mind was drawing me closer to this Jesus who had captured my wife's heart. Chris was in chemotherapy for three months when she was hospitalized with Pneumocistis Carnii, a type of pneumonia that can strike leukemia patients. She went into the hospital, and soon her pneumonia progressed to the point where she was placed in intensive care. Her condition grew progressively worse. They put her on a ventilator because her lungs were so filled with disease.

Bad News

During those days visitor privileges were limited to a few minutes every so many hours. The doctors tried every drug imaginable to clear Chris's lungs, but her condition continued to deteriorate. At the intensive care entrance, nurses would not make eye contact with us because they knew Chris was dying. It was at that point that I turned to Jan and said, "If Chris dies, I will never accept it." Her breathing was hard, rapid, and labored; it sounded like she had just finished running a record-breaking marathon. That evening in the intensive care waiting room, Dr. Schwartz told us they had just taken another

X-ray and it showed that Chris's lungs were literally black; air was just bouncing off of them. He said it was just a matter of time before her heart gave out. Death was imminent.

Miracle Number One

We had noticed that Dr. Lee was conspicuously missing. Later on, we learned that he was so distraught over her condition that he temporarily removed himself from her case. Jan went to the chapel and surrendered Chris and herself to Jesus. During the early-morning hours, Dr. Schwartz woke us up in the intensive care waiting room to inform us that they had taken another X-ray and it showed a "pin like" opening in Chris's lungs. It was a positive sign but not a big one. The next morning we visited Chris in intensive care and she was slightly better. In a few short hours, she officially turned the corner and came off the ventilator. Dr. Schwartz told us she might be in the hospital a maximum of two months before she could go home. In less than forty-eight hours, Chris was sitting up in her bed and requested a TV so she could watch *Happy Days*. Within two weeks, she was home riding her bike. We had needed a miracle, and boy, did we get one!

A Doctor Shared

During Chris's recovery, Jan met one of the doctors in the elevator, and he asked her if she was Christine Carr's mother. Jan acknowledged that she was, and the doctor continued, "I just wanted you to know you have a special daughter. We had over fifty doctors across the country working on your daughter's case, and nothing we did medically saved her. She received a miracle." The doctor's comments definitely caught my attention.

Getting My Attention

Chris's miracle drew me closer in my search for God. I realized that what had taken place in that hospital a few days earlier was more than a coincidence; something supernatural had occurred. Life for us returned to normal (whatever that meant) in our household. Chris returned to school and continued her regular visits to Children's Memorial Hospital for checkups. I cannot put into words how good it felt to relax and enjoy family life together. This relatively stress-free time allowed me to explore the faith. I became more than a casual observer of Jan's newfound peace and joy.

The Quest for Truth

I wanted to believe in some supernatural power beyond myself. Deep in my heart I knew there was more to life than our current existence. However, I held on to a vague understanding of God's creation account as recorded in Genesis, the first book in the Bible. I guess I believed God created the heavens and the earth. I guess God formed the earth out of nothing. I guess God spoke light into the earth and His spirit was hovering over the waters. I guess God separated light from darkness and created all the birds that flew across the sky and animals that roamed the land. I guess God made human beings in His own image. I guess God did all this and more in seven twenty-four-hour days.

Jesus Who?

I must be honest. I did not know where the four Gospels were in the New Testament. I had very little understanding of their content. I knew Jesus was part of the story, but that was about the extent of my biblical knowledge at the time. If you would have told me back then that the four Gospels presented the person, work, miracles, teachings, betrayal, crucifixion, and resurrection of Jesus Christ, I would have responded with a blank look and a surprised "Oh really?"

Ripe for Spiritual Pickings

Unbeknownst to me, God was preparing my heart for a marvelous revelation of His Son Jesus Christ and a thirst and hunger for His mighty Word. I was ripe and ready for what was to come spiritually. But I had not yet grasped the real significance of this sentence: *being committed and obedient to God's commands are what Jesus and His Word demands*. This was a divine mandate that I just did not care to learn or affirm before my search for the real Jesus found in the Bible.

The Cream of the Crop

It never dawned on me that I could know this Creator of the universe personally. I never fully appreciated the magnitude of what it meant that we are made in His image. Not only are we custom-made physically, but God has also uniquely shaped our personalities, minds, wills, and emotions, and given us the incredible gift of choice. We have the freedom to either accept or reject His love for us in Christ. We are His special creation. These truths were just foreign to me.

Searching in All the Wrong Places

In those early years in my life and marriage, I understood that God existed somewhere out there. However, the idea of having some kind of intimate relationship with Him was certainly not part of my worldview. I was looking for contentment, purpose, strength, and direction in what this material world had to offer instead of God. For me, God was some kind of distant mystical figure. I was trying to make sense of and come to terms with Chris's illness from a human perspective, and God was not the answer. I lacked the knowledge to apply this truth: *trusting God can turn your devastation into holy preservation*. I was at a bad place. My life had become an absolute train wreck. I was pretty much a mental and emotional basket case and spiritually bankrupt.

The Search Goes On

In spite of my dazed and confused state, I kept searching for God to help me make sense of the turmoil that was dominating my energies, thoughts, and actions. Each day I would ask Jan probing questions about her faith. I was intrigued by how well she was handling our chaotic lives. She seemed to be in control, filled with confidence and peace about our daughter's physical condition. She had something within that I did not have. Then one night I decided it was time for a showdown.

I asked Jan how God gave her the strength to deal with Chris's illness and at the same time maintain stability in our household. I was just blown away by her faith. I wanted what she had. I wanted to experience peace and hope for myself. I wanted to be able to turn to someone, something, a greater higher power, so I could cope with our tragic events. I was crying out for help, but I did not understand how to attain the love, strength, and comfort I was so desperately searching for.

The Big Moment Draws Near

Finally, one evening when the girls were in bed, I once again approached Jan. She shared how Jesus Christ had turned her life around, and how He gave her guidance, courage, and hope to live every day. Jan shared how her friend Sandy had led her to Christ. When Jesus came into her heart, Jan's whole outlook on life changed. Her steady calmness in the midst of the storm could not be denied. I knew God had done something special in her life, and I wanted what she had! So I asked Jan if I could know Jesus the way she knew Him. She encouraged me to read the gospel of John from the perspective of it having been written just for me.

Ready for the Launch

I spent the next few days reading John's gospel with Jan's suggestion in mind. While reading verse after verse, chapter after chapter, story after story, parable after parable, miracle after miracle, and about healing after healing, Jesus became more and more personal to me. I no longer viewed Him as some distant Savior. The more I read, the more the Word of God came alive in me. I was ripe for a Spiritual encounter, a special touch from the Master, Jesus Himself. With every word I read, I became increasingly intrigued with Jesus of Nazareth. Jan's and Chris's faith began to grow stronger every day.

My Approach to the Throne

When I finished reading John's gospel, I asked Jan what I needed to do to receive Jesus as my personal Lord and Savior. She simply advised me to go upstairs in our bedroom, and pray and say to Jesus, "If You are who You say You are, come into my heart and reveal Yourself to me." She told me that He wouldn't let me down. Like an obedient husband, I listened to her advice. The author of Hebrews writes, "Therefore, since the promise of entering His rest still stands, let us be careful that none of you be found to have fallen short of it. For we also have had the Gospel preached to us, just as they did; but the message they heard was of no value to them, because those who heard did not combine it with faith" (Hebrews 4:1-2).

In the days of Moses, God promised the people of Israel a time of rest in the midst of their problems. Unfortunately, they were disobedient. They did not take God up on His promises. They knew about

God, but they did not have a heart for Him. They did not put their knowledge of God into action. I decided to challenge God and His promise of rest in the midst of my trials. I wanted to rid myself of my old ways and experience God's promises in Christ.

Seeking Love and Truth

In verses 14-16 we read, "Therefore, since we have a great high priest who has gone through the Heavens, Jesus the Son of God, let us hold firmly to the faith we profess. For we do not have a high priest who is unable to sympathize with our weaknesses, but we have one who has been tempted in every way, just as we are—yet was without sin. Let us then approach the throne of grace with confidence, so that we may receive mercy and find grace to help us in our time of need."

These verses remind us that Jesus, our High Priest, knows about our warts, weaknesses, frailties, and temptations. When trials and testing come into our lives, we can turn to the throne of grace and find the help and strength only Jesus can provide. I had a hunger and thirst to rest on the throne of Jesus' love. I wanted to embrace His love, grace, truth, and promises.

I went into my bedroom, and like in verse 16, I approached the throne of grace, not sure of or confident about what to expect. All I cared about was quenching my thirst to experience Jesus' presence with all my heart, body, and soul. I fell to my knees and prayed, "Jesus, if you are who You say You are, come into my heart. I receive You now as my Lord and Savior."

Miracle Number Two

The moment I finished praying that prayer, it was Spiritual bells and whistles! It was Fourth of July fireworks! In an instant my life changed. Alone in that room, Jesus turned me inside out. I was a new person. God changed my values and the way I looked at life. The Spirit of God filled me with a deeper love for my family. In an instant my view of the world changed. I wasn't the same person who had entered that bedroom a short time earlier. Jesus gave me a new purpose, a new perspective, and a new point of view. The love and presence of Christ completely changed me. From that day on, my life would never be the same. What I had needed was a miracle, and I got one big time! This is what the apostle Paul wrote in Second Corinthians: "Therefore, if anyone is in Christ, he is a new creation; the old has gone, the new has come" (2 Corinthians 5:17).

My New Friend

I had found a new friend who would walk with me through all the tests and trials that would come our way. Jesus is a living, active Lord who would provide victory even in the most horrible circumstances, a Lord who would supply all our needs, a Lord who would give us comfort and supernatural strength in the days and years to come. I walked into that bedroom confused, searching for a friend, trying to find the God of all creation who would journey with my family and me every single day. Without a doubt, I left that bedroom a changed man. It finally made sense what Jan was saying all along about her new life in Christ. A Christian song from the seventies would become my theme song from that day forth. Some of the lyrics said, "I have a friend I want you to know, He's always there wherever you go. He's always there I want you to know." All I had needed was a miracle, and I had found my miracle in Jesus. I had become a new creation in Christ and it felt great. It is so true: *Jesus can turn your tribulation into jubilation!*

Jesus can remove your duress and give you success.

"Sweet Caroline"
Words by: Neil Diamond
(Some lyrics paraphrased)

I cannot begin to know when you came along.
Those times when we held hands felt so good
The pain and hurt of lonely nights didn't seem so bad
When I embraced you.
Our time together has been so good
And I believe they always will.

CHAPTER FOUR

"Sweet Caroline"

Let the Good Times Roll

As I said in the last chapter, I was spiritually washed from the inside out. My cup was literally overflowing with the very Spirit and presence of Christ. I was emotionally and mentally higher than a kite. God was all over me, and I was just soaking it all in. I don't know exactly how long I was in that bedroom, but I didn't care. I did not want to leave! I had fallen passionately in love with Jesus Christ, King of Kings and Lord of Lords. What I felt and experienced was real, not fantasy or wishful thinking. Then it was time to leave my sacred place.

Say What?

What had taken place in my upper room was biblically driven through and through. Paul said these life-changing words: "That if you confess with your mouth, Jesus is Lord, and believe in your heart that God raised Him from the dead, you will be saved" (Romans 10:9). Paul makes our salvation easy to understand and accept. God is not hanging out in the heavens somewhere, millions of light-years away. He is as close to you as your heart. God is so near that if you stopped walking, you would bump into Him. In other words, finding salvation in Christ is as near as the confession that rolls off your tongue. Salvation comes to those who confess that Jesus is Lord and believe in their hearts that Jesus Christ was crucified, buried, and raised from the dead. God made salvation simple, yet we often make it complicated.

Paul continues, "As the Scripture says, anyone who trusts in Him will never be put to shame" (Romans 10:11). When I entered my bedroom to find Jesus, the human side of me was reluctant, skeptical because my life was spiraling downward big time. Was Jan's Jesus too good to be really true? Would I be disappointed? Would God disappoint me? I had many questions and not enough answers. Paul reminds us that God is not out to play games with us. He always keeps His promises. We can trust that God will do what He says He will do. We need to understand that God will never lie, nor will He renege on His promises. Without a doubt life will always bring its own set of problems, and Christians are not exempt from them. However, God will keep His promises. He will save every person regardless of their past. If they will "call upon the Lord Jesus Christ they will be saved," according to Romans 19:13. People and circumstances will let us down from time to time, but Jesus will never let us down. He is constant day in and day out. The writer of Hebrews confirms this: "Never will I leave you; never will I forsake you" (Hebrews 13:8).

Coming Down the Mountain

I had spent a glorious time on my mount of transformation. There in my room I met the divine three-in-one God, Jesus, and the Holy Spirit. That was truly a God moment! Jesus confirmed my encounter with Him when He said, "But you will receive power when the Holy Spirit comes on you; and you will be my witnesses in Jerusalem, and in all Judea and Samaria, and to the ends of the earth" (Acts 1:8). After His resurrection, Jesus appeared to His disciples before He ascended into heaven. Jesus told them He would no longer be with them physically. However, He would send His Holy Spirit to empower them to serve and share the testimony of Christ. The gospel would be spread throughout the world and history by the transforming power of the Holy Spirit. The Holy Spirit gives all Christians the courage, insight, wisdom, tools, and ability to know Jesus personally and let Him be known. Therefore, if any person has received Jesus into his or her heart as Lord and Savior, then His Holy Spirit, the very power of God, fills them. If the power of Jesus is in us, we can do extraordinary things in this life. Now it was time to leave the joy of my holy (bedroom) mountain.

I Feel Strong Now

I bolted out of my bedroom and bounded down the stairs, movin' and groovin' with my arms flapping and feet flopping like John Travolta in *Saturday Night Fever*. I felt invincible in the Lord. There was not a mountain too large or treacherous that I could not climb. My attitude was thanking the Lord for the nighttime and forgetting the day's troubles. My spiritual fire was lit, and no one and no situation was going to put it out! Consider what Paul said: "And you also were included in Christ when you heard the word of truth, the gospel of your salvation. Having believed, you were marked in Him, with a seal, the promised Holy Spirit, who is a deposit guaranteeing our inheritance until the redemption of those who are God's possession—to the praise of His glory" (Ephesians 1:13-14). These verses remind us that the Spirit of God fills a heart the very moment one receives Jesus as Lord and Savior. The Holy Spirit is God's guarantee, promise, and seal that every born-again believer belongs to God and nothing will be able to separate him or her from the love of God in Christ.

The Real Deal

My spiritual eyes and heart were opened. I discovered many nuggets of truth that night—mainly that I was now a child of the living

Christ. The Spirit of God gave me extraordinary confidence in Jesus' presence within my being. I knew my salvation was real. I couldn't explain it, and I couldn't contain it, and I didn't want to. I had had a divine encounter like the one recorded in the book of Acts: "Salvation is found in no one else, for there is no other name under Heaven given to men by which we must be saved" (Acts 4:12). Here Peter offered the Jews a "Billy Graham moment" by encouraging them to receive Jesus Christ as Savior. This was one of the early New Testament altar calls.

Let Jesus Come In

Our society at large rejects Acts 4:12, simply because it makes followers of many religions and some in Christian circles uncomfortable with its claim that there is no other name than Jesus' that we can call on to be saved. They say this is a bold and arrogant statement. Friends, I don't make the rules, you don't make the rules, and humanity does not make the rules regarding our eternal destination. Only God does, through the Bible. This is a mandate from the Almighty God Himself. If God says Jesus is the only way to salvation, then let it be so. *Therefore, just relax and go with His Spiritual flow.*

It Is What It Is

God has no equal; we cannot make up our pet theologies as we go along to fit our personal biases. The gospel of John reads, "Jesus answered, I am the way the truth, and the life. No one comes to the Father except through Me" (John 14:6). Jesus made a bold proclamation when He said, "I am the way." He meant there is only one road that leads to God. Jesus is our one-way street to the Father. Then Jesus said, "I am the truth." This revelation represents God's greatest attributes and biblical truth (God never lies). Finally Jesus said, "and the life." As believers in Jesus, we become children of God. Through His Spirit we gain access to His divine character both now and forever.

Bounding Love, Joy, and Confidence

That night when I met Jan in our kitchen, I was a new spiritual man. The cross and the power of the resurrection had redeemed me. No other religion can make that claim. I received forgiveness for my sins. I had been set free from my past, and the Holy Spirit gave me a clean slate, all because of the covenant of our Lord's grace and love. Jesus offered me a life that I could not reject. For the first time I could honestly say life was good! Jesus had profoundly touched me, and forgave all my past transgressions through His sacrificial death on the cross, and I was liberated. John said these life-changing words: "If we confess our sins, He is faithful and just and will forgive us our sins and purify us from all unrighteousness" (1 John 1:9).

An Overflowing Love

I accepted Jesus' offer by faith, a faith that had been planted in my heart and mind. My cup had surely overflowed with love, joy, and confidence. It all happened because I fell to my knees and prayed. In the classic Irving Berlin movie *White Christmas*, Danny Kaye sings, "The best things happen when you're dancing." I believe the best things happen when we pray!

Sharing with Jan in our kitchen that night was just awesome. It felt like the weight of our troubles had been lifted off my shoulders. I had a peace and blessed assurance that I had never encountered in my life. I reached out for the heart of Christ, and He touched me in a most wonderful, dynamic way. Galatians reads, "Before this faith came, we were held prisoners by the law, locked up until faith should be revealed. So the law was put in charge to lead us to Christ that we might be justified by faith. Now that faith has come, we are no longer under the supervision of the law" (Galatians 3:23-25).

Free at Last

This passage reminds us that God gave the Jews the law, the Ten Commandments, as boundaries in terms of how to live. They also pointed out humanity's flaws and sins, and God's desire to forgive us. In other words, God gave us the Ten Commandments to show us our failures and shortcomings and that we will never measure up through our own efforts. The Old Testament principles still apply in the twenty-first century. God has revealed His perfect nature, His moral laws, and standards for living a righteous life. But we need to remember that simply living a moral life and obeying all the rules will not save us. Only Christ can save us and remove our sin. The law simply paved the way for finding redemption in Christ.

All Ready but Not Yet

One reality I have learned from my new life in Christ is that I am still susceptible to sin. From time to time my humanness gets in the way; I do, say, or think things that are not pleasing to the Lord and others. There are moments when we fall into temptation and sin. One of my New Testament professors at Northern Theological Seminary used to say, "We are all ready but not yet." His point was that as believers in Christ, we are already redeemed. Our eternal destination and salvation is secure, but we are not yet—meaning that as Christians, we are still on our journey to the promised land of heaven. This means we are still subject to the sinful ways of this corrupt world.

Getting in the Groove

After Jan and I experienced a radical conversion, our faith grew dramatically. We daily saturated ourselves in the Word. Biblical truths were coming alive in us. After my dramatic encounter with the Lord, I began attending church with Jan and the girls. I could not wait for Sunday services. I became involved with a men's group that met before the early-morning Sunday worship service. We started attending adult Sunday school and Bible studies. We just couldn't wait to share what Jesus had done in our lives. As the song goes, we were growing strong, and the "good times never seemed so good."

Lock Us Up

I guess it was safe to say we became fanatics for Christ in those early days at Fox Valley Presbyterian Church in Geneva. Perhaps we took our spiritual fervor to such an extreme that some in our church considered us obnoxious and even spiritually dangerous. We could not contain our faith; the spiritual fire within us could not be quenched. We genuinely believed God had given us deep spiritual wisdom. Our confidence was sky high. We felt we could handle the tough spiritual questions and developed a "bring-it-on" attitude. One would have had to put us in chains and sewed our lips shut to keep us silent. There wasn't a doubt we were operating on high spiritual octane.

Expanding Our Boundaries

Without question, God had put us on a crash course in the faith. Jan began leading a neighborhood women's prayer group. God showed up in mighty ways during their prayer sessions. They witnessed many supernatural manifestations of the Holy Spirit, to the point where I couldn't wait for Jan to share what God had done at their latest prayer meeting. This prayer group would become very instrumental in building Jan's faith and preparing her for the events that were to come. God was surely putting our faith on speed dial. We attended spiritual conferences throughout our communities. Attending special ministry opportunities at Calvary Church in Naperville, Illinois, played a crucial role in our early faith walk. Jesus was active and on the move, not only in our family life but also in the lives of our Christian friends.

Family Time

Shortly after our spiritual awakening, we initiated evening devotionals with our girls. We felt this was a great time to mold and build a solid foundation in the faith for our children. God truly blessed our family devotional time together. Obviously we kept it simple to match their level of understanding. We told them Bible stories and had Bible quizzes: Name the four Gospels. Who parted the Red Sea? Who was called the father of the faith? And so on.

It was amazing how astute the girls grew in the fundamentals of the Bible. It was during those evenings of sharing that each one of our children gave her life to Christ. Those little evening devotionals were certainly more than worth it. What a privilege it was to see our children's lives being transformed in Christ every day.

Boldness Revealed

God was blessing us beyond measure. Chris was doing fine; her leukemia was in remission. However, the threat of this terrible disease still lingered in our minds. We decided to be more honest and straightforward with Chris about her diagnosis and about what God had miraculously done when she was fighting pneumonia. School had just begun when one of Chris's classmates told her she would be "dead by Christmas." I will never forget the defiant look in Chris's blue eyes when I asked how she had replied. She told the little girl, "No way am I going to die." That was the first of many signs of the faith and fighting spirit that Chris would demonstrate in dealing with her disease.

Hold On

We had learned early on what Jesus meant when He said, "So do not worry, saying, what shall we eat? Or what shall we drink? Or what shall we wear? For the pagans run after all these things and your Heavenly Father knows that you need them. But seek first His Kingdom and His righteousness, and all these things will be given to you as well. Therefore, do not worry about tomorrow, for tomorrow will worry about itself. Each day has enough trouble of its own" (Matthew 6:31–34). We were learning to live one day at a time. We were holding on to Christ with every ounce of faith we had. Jesus was reminding us that worrying about the things of this world only leads to frustration. It's foolish to worry about things that are here today and gone tomorrow. True meaning in life goes far beyond food and clothing.

Quiet Assurance

Christ assures us that we are more valuable than what nature provides. God cares for the needs of nature, yet He cares far more for us, His special creation. God knows exactly what we need for each day. If we put Him first, He will meet our every need according to His grace and mercy.

Someone once said, "Planning for tomorrow is time well spent; worrying about tomorrow is time wasted." Each day we were learning how to trust and obey God in every decision, every test, every pain, and every tear. We were lifting our worries for the day, the week, and the month up to God. Every time we did, Jesus came through.

Comfort from Within

The power and presence of Christ filled us with His loving comfort. During this period, our nights were not consumed with fear, anxiety, or loneliness. The Lord's strength and tender care replaced our pain.

Following Jesus keeps us from going astray.

"I Will Follow Him"
Words by: Franck Pourcel and Paul Mauriat
(Some lyrics paraphrased)

My love for him goes so deep that I will follow him
Wherever he may be, neither ocean nor mountain
Can keep me from his presence.
He will be my one and only love forever.

CHAPTER FIVE

"I Will Follow Him"

Keep the Faith

My coming to Christ and our family's increased involvement in church began during the 1974 Christmas holiday season. Chris's leukemia had been diagnosed a few months earlier. She had survived almost certain death. Jan's and my conversions to the Lord set the tone for all our future experiences, which included "the good, the bad, and the ugly." Yes, this was our first Christmas in the faith. The traditional Christmas carol's words "Joy to the world, the Lord is come" took on a new and deeper meaning for us. We were no longer facing the trials and tribulations of Chris's illness alone and in desperation. Faith became our constant refuge and strength.

Keep It Simple

The writer of Hebrews wrote, "Now faith is being sure of what we hope for and certain of what we do not see. This is what the ancients were commended for. By faith we understand that the universe was formed at God's command, so that what is seen was not made out of what was invisible" (Hebrews 11:1-3). A childlike, uninhibited faith accompanied us. We simply expected God to surprise us with His presence every day. Our new faith just excited us; we were wired for Christ. The Holy Spirit brought us into a marvelous supernatural intervention of God's grace, power, and promise. We lived those days with a sense of wonder based on the anticipation that God would deliver. We loved Him, we loved Him, and wherever He went, we would follow!

Basically, this is what verses 1–3 imply. The Bible assures us that what God has done in the past He will also do in the present and future for all who call upon the name of the Lord Jesus Christ. God is faithful. He will always come through. There are times when we don't get it or even agree with what God is doing. Regardless, we can trust that He is in control and knows what is best for us no matter the situation. What happens in this world does not catch God by surprise.

Being Sure and Certain

One interpretation of Hebrews 11:1 says this verse associates faith with two key words: *sure* and *certain*. The starting point of faith is to believe and be sure that God is who He says He is. The ending point is being certain that God will deliver whatever He promises. Therefore, taking God at His word is all the proof we really need. When we embrace what God says in His Word, His Holy Spirit will give us all the assurance and confidence of knowing He will work out all things for our good, according to Romans 8:28.

This kind of faith influenced my life. It wasn't a faith based on emotional, warm and fuzzy feelings or believe-what-you-want-to-believe theology. I was absolutely sure and certain that "all Scripture was inspired" by the Holy Spirit of God. If God said it, I believed it; thus let it be so. Hebrews 11:6 was at the core of my faith walk: "And without faith it is impossible to please God, because anyone who comes to Him must believe He exists and that He rewards those who earnestly seek Him." True faith goes beyond intellectual general knowledge of God's existence. A live faith comes only when Jesus Christ comes into a person's heart.

You Can't Take It with You

Faith carries with it eternal ramifications. However, the values of this world tell us that money, status, getting ahead, and being popular, good looking, and intelligent are all the qualities you need to achieve ultimate happiness and contentment in this life. One can be buried in a custom-made Natalia SLS 2 (2007) designed by Alfred Di Mora for approximately two million dollars! But you can't drive that car out of the grave and drive it down the paved streets of heaven. We can't take into eternity all the things we have acquired in this world.

The Unfading Word

Let's pay some attention to the following words from First Peter: "For you have been born again, not of perishable seed, but of imperishable, through the living and enduring Word of God. For, all men are like grass, and all their glory is like the flowers of the field, the grass withers and the flowers fall, but the Word of the Lord stands forever. And this is the Word that was preached to you" (1 Peter 1:23–25). It doesn't matter if we have a luxury car worth millions or are financially secure; Peter reminds us that everything created by the flesh in this life will one day disappear. Seeds that are planted in the soil will produce certain fruits, grass, and flowers; all will endure for a season. It's also true that seeds from God's Word that are planted in one's heart and mind will not end but will last through eternity.

Looking to Him

Even when fear clouded our daughter's future, with all the uncertainties looming over us, we discovered the key to living a truly abundant life. We were learning how to persevere by fixing our eyes on

Jesus, being obedient, and applying the imperishable Word of God to our daily lives. Hebrews reads,

> Therefore, since we are surrounded by such a great crowd of witnesses (Champions of the faith), let us throw off everything that hinders and the sin that so easily entangles, and let us run with perseverance the race marked out for us. Let us fix our eyes on Jesus, the author and perfecter of our faith, who for the joy set before Him endured the cross, scorning its shame, and sat down at the right hand of the throne of God. Consider Him who endured such opposition from sinful men, so that you will not grow weary and lose heart. In your struggle against sin, you have not yet resisted to the point of shedding your blood. (Hebrews 12:1-4)

Our Guiding Light

I'm writing this because it is important for every reader of this book to understand that the light of Jesus was guiding us every step along the way. We literally held on to His Word every day. Without Jesus, and the sustaining power of His word, we would have crashed and burned emotionally, psychologically, and spiritually. My prayer is that you will come to the same conclusion regardless of your struggles, and that Jesus will be there for you.

Being a Role Model

As Jan and I grew in our daily walk with Christ, we wanted our children to embrace Jesus' love and compassion in their own way. We believed this was crucial for maintaining consistency and balance in our family life. The Bible challenges us to be examples for others. Paul said, "Follow my example, as I follow the example of Christ. I praise you for remembering me in everything and for holding to the teachings, just as I passed them on to you" (1 Corinthians 11:1-2). Paul wanted the Corinthians to follow His example because he wanted them to understand the faith and take their worship seriously. It was also our desire for our children to grow in their faith and take Jesus seriously. What better way for this to happen than for Mom and Dad to model genuine trust in Jesus?

Don't Mess with My Money!

You can kick my dog.

You can despise me.

You can scorn me.

You can degrade me.

You can steal my car.

You can trash my reputation.

You can insult my friends.

I can handle all the pain.

However, there is one thing you cannot do: mess with my money!

Friends, that seems to be our culture's mantra these days.

The point I'm trying to make is obvious. Actor Tom Cruise played the role as a sports agent in the movie *Jerry McGuire*. The phrase "show me the money" became the centerpiece for the movie. The *Wall Street Journal* has become our society's financial Bible. Our modern society covets making money, saving money, and spending money. Our culture has this unquenchable thirst for money and lots of it. For many people, money has become their God. *The love and lust for money can burn a hole in your soul.*

Facing the Music

A time will come in every Christian's life when he or she must give an account and face his or her financial stewardship responsibility. Giving money to our Lord and His work should be considered both an opportunity and a privilege. Financial giving offers every believer the opportunity to serve not only God but also others. We should not give because somebody puts the squeeze on us to do so. We don't give simply to impress or to compare ourselves with others. No, our motive for giving, be it of our time, talents, or finances, should be out of our love and gratitude for what God has done for us in Christ. Besides, it's biblical.

A Commitment to Give

Jan's and my financial giving became very important early in our Christian walk. It would become crucial to our spiritual growth and living out our faith every day. If we could trust God for our daughter's well-being, then why couldn't we trust Him for our financial well-being? We simply put our trust in all His provisions. We didn't wait to make a financial commitment after we were free from our financial burdens. The Bible tells us that when we give out of our love and reverence for Christ, we will also receive blessings. It was up to us; it was our choice to make.

God Does Not Want Our Leftovers

> Remember this: Whoever sows sparingly will also reap sparingly, and whoever sows generously will also reap generously. Each man should give what he has decided in his heart to give, not reluctantly or under compulsion, for God loves a cheerful giver. And God is able to make all grace abound to you, so that in all things at all times, having all that you need, you will abound in every good

work. He has scattered abroad His gifts to the poor, His righteousness endures forever. (2 Corinthians 9:6-9)

Paul was saying that if we are faithful in our giving, God will bless and be faithful to us. God is not so much concerned about the amount we give but how we give. He wants our giving to come from our hearts. It is uplifting, and it feels good and joyful when we give to God with the right attitude. Notice the series of phrases Paul used in this passage: His grace will abound in you, all things, all needs, and every good work. It is God's desire to provide for us in every circumstance.

This passage from Luke gives the reader a clearer picture of how we depended on the Lord for meeting all our needs even in our sacrificial giving. The Word of God set the spiritual tone for the many blessings we received from the hand of God. We merely put our trust in Jesus' promise when He said, "Give, and it will be given to you. A good measure, pressed down, shaken together and running over, will be poured into your lap. For with the measure you use, it will be measured to you" (Luke 6:38). Early on in our faith walk, we practiced obedience and learned to follow Jesus in all things, even in our giving.

Faith in Jesus today gives us hope for tomorrow.

"Day by Day"
Words by: Stephen Schwartz (New Music)
(Some lyrics paraphrased)

Every day, Lord, I will lift up these three promises.
That I may keep You in my view.
That my love for You will grow deeper.
That I will remain close to You.
Each and every day.

CHAPTER SIX

"Day by Day"

Follow the Leader

As we started to grow in our newfound faith, we learned quickly how necessary it was to seek and follow the Lord every day. There were three things we prayed for in our walk with Christ: 1) that our vision for Jesus would be keen; 2) that our love for Jesus would grow deeper; and 3) that we would remain close to Him every day. Jesus said, "My prayer is not that You take them out of the world but that You protect them from the evil one. They are not of the world, even as I am not of it. Sanctify them by the truth; Your Word is truth" (John 17:15-17).

Jesus was praying for His disciples but also for all believers past, present, and future. A key word is found in verse 17: *sanctification.* Jesus wanted His followers to understand that they were sanctified (set apart) for divine purposes through the word. Jesus was not talking about Christians becoming perfect without sin. Jan and I were in the process of being sanctified. Each day we were growing in the Lord by reading, praying, and applying His Word. Jesus was refining us, setting us apart, and moving us closer and closer to Almighty God.

The Word of Truth

God's Word had such an effect on us because we had come to the realization that the Bible was not like any other book. Reading the Bible goes beyond simply reading words on a page. It is God's revelation to us! It's not just another book that we should casually gloss over. The Bible comes alive when we read and apply its truths, lessons, teachings, miracles, and promises to our lives. That is when real Christian living and enjoying the abundant life really begins. Proverbs reads, "Your Word is a lamp to my feet and a light for my path" (Proverbs 119:105). *The light of God's Word shows us the way every single day.*

Feeling Mighty Fine

It felt great being loved by God and walking in His presence. Our commitment to embracing the authority of Scripture and seeking to be obedient to its instruction, correction, and direction definitely had a cleansing effect on our hearts. Although Chris's illness was constantly on our minds, we knew without a doubt that God would never leave or forsake us. We believed Jesus was the great healer. Life for us had never felt better spiritually. While still subject to the world's limitations, the Carr family was now marching to a different drummer: Jesus, the one who said, "But take heart! I have overcome the world" (John 16:33).

Life Just Doesn't Get Any Better Than This

It is hard to put into words how good life was for us during that period of time. The power of the living Christ raised the bar of our enthusiasm dramatically. We yearned for more faith in and power from the Lord. In our darkest hour, as scared, confused, and traumatized young parents trying to cope with a terminally ill child, we reached out to our living God. Wow, did He deliver big time! I believe divine encouragement and true contentment in Christ comes to us by way of sincere humility. In James we read, "Humble yourselves before the Lord, and He will lift you up" (James 4:10).

Get Over Yourself

Humility can be a real big character bender. James warns against a huge problem that confronts every person who walks on this earth: pride. Spiritual pride depends on self and does not acknowledge one's need for God's intervention. It's the "me, myself, and I" syndrome. Pride puts distance between God and us. When a Christian comes to the cross in true humility, the believer learns a crucial ingredient for living out everyday faith. He or she cannot survive without the intervention of God's help, mercy, power, and compassion.

Cruising Along

After Chris's bout with pneumonia, life was going well for the Carr family. Chris was in remission and back in school. Connie and Diane were adjusting to Chris's illness. As a family, we were content with the place our faith had in our lives. Jan was running the house, keeping us in order. I was busy with my job at Jewel Food Stores. Even our dog was enjoying the relaxed atmosphere. We were like regular folks, doing normal things that normal families do, and it sure felt good. To top it all off, our faith was growing by leaps and bounds. What a blessing it was to witness Jesus' love and presence filling our amazing little girls day by day.

Bold and Daring

God seemed to have our faith walk on fast forward. We were in awe of how God was revealing new truths to us through the Word every day. God was giving us a clearer picture of His will and purpose for our lives. He was teaching, challenging, and nurturing us by His Word. Confidence and boldness in the saving knowledge of Jesus just oozed in our veins. The Holy Spirit of God was all over us; we felt almost invincible and indestructible. *Placing our lives under Jesus' control kept us on a spiritual roll* best describes the condition of our faith in those days.

Lessons to Be Learned

There was no doubt that at the time, our confidence in the faith bordered on the arrogant and obnoxious. Paul wrote, "It is because of Him that you are in Christ Jesus, who has become for us wisdom of God-that is, our righteousness, holiness and redemption. Therefore, as it is written: let him who boasts boast in the Lord" (1 Corinthians 1:31). Paul stresses the importance of knowing that simple faith, not human wisdom, is central to salvation. Our salvation is totally Christ centered, not human centered. Jesus is all we will ever need. He is our Lord, our Savior, our righteousness, and our wisdom, period.

Wrong Thinking

To add to what Christ has already done for us through His life, suffering, crucifixion, and resurrection is to diminish His divine work. When this happens, we tend to boast about our knowledge and wisdom instead of boasting about what Jesus alone can do. We were still babes in Christ, but we thought we were way ahead of the spiritual curve. There were moments when we believed that we had all the deep answers to the faith for almost any situation. However, God was about to teach us another life lesson.

Spiritual Hotshots

We were getting too big for our spiritual britches and began tossing all conventional wisdom out the window, because we thought God worked only in the realm of the supernatural. We believed that those who did not affirm our beliefs were spiritually weak and lacked Holy Spirit insight. Scary, isn't it? Nevertheless that was our mind-set. How could God ever get anything done without our help and wisdom? We were strutting around thinking we must be God's special cream of the crop, the best of the best.

Considering the Options

Chris was doing so well, our confidence in God's power and intervention was off the charts. We were following Jesus day by day. At one of Chris's regular checkups, the oncology staff at Children's Memorial Hospital presented us with an additional treatment option. They concluded from the latest research that Chris's current treatment of intrathecal spinal chemotherapy wasn't as effective as radiation. The daily dose of radiation for six weeks Monday through Friday at Wesley Memorial Hospital in Chicago would be the best option for her. They told us that the radiation would cause her hair to fall out.

Should We or Shouldn't We?

We told the hospital staff we needed to pray and think about their suggested treatment. For the next few days we struggled with the doctor's recommendation. The idea of radiation just did not resonate with us. In our minds they were trying to change the game plan. We kept vacillating: yes, we should; no, we shouldn't. James wrote,

> If any of you lacks wisdom, he should ask God, who gives generously to all without finding fault, and it will be given

to him. But when he asks, he must believe and not doubt, because he who doubts is like a wave of the sea, blown and tossed by the wind. That man should not think he will receive anything from the Lord; he is a double-minded man, unstable in all he does. (James 1:5–8)

The Heat Is On

This was the first pressure-filled decision surrounding Chris's illness we would have to make from a faith perspective. We lifted this difficult problem up to God in prayer. We were confused and frustrated. James reminds us that we can pray and ask God for His wisdom, and He will give it to us. However, we will miss His wisdom if our motives are self-centered and not Jesus centered. To believe and not doubt is to lay one's trust at Jesus' feet, knowing He will meet the need, whatever it is. Conversely, a vacillating person is not totally sold out and does not trust that God has the best solution. Doubt leaves a person anxious and unsure, like unsettled ocean waves that roll in and go out. Placing our faith in an unshakable, all-knowing God, who knows what is best for us regardless of the circumstances, always leads to His peace and stability.

The Showdown

A short time later, we had an appointment to discuss radiation treatment with Chris's lead doctor, Dr. Lee. Yes, we prayed, but we were still unsure. So we took matters into our own hands. Since God had miraculously healed Chris of a deadly form of pneumonia a few months earlier, we just assumed He could and would do it again! Therefore, we firmly believed Chris did not need the radiation. It was "high noon," with us against Dr. Lee. We thought we were the good guys and would be victorious because God's righteousness was on our side. There we were, face to face with Dr. Lee in his office.

The confrontation had arrived. The atmosphere was tense. What side would start pleading their case first? We sat down and stared at Dr. Lee, who was sitting behind his desk a few steps away. We believed our ultimate weapon was God. In the Old Testament Habakkuk wrote, "See, he is puffed up; his desires are not upright—but the righteous will live by his faith" (Habakkuk 2:4).

Words of Wisdom

In this passage the cruel and ruthless Babylonians were extremely confident in their abilities. They didn't need the hand of God in their lives because they were so full of their own sense of right and power. Jan and I lacked a clear understanding of this passage from Habakkuk and confronted this doctor spiritually puffed up. We told Dr. Lee our decision was not to pursue radiation for Chris. We believed God had already healed her; therefore radiation treatment wasn't necessary. Dr. Lee sat there and looked concerned but listened patiently. After we finished, he responded in a strong and forceful professional tone, "Don't you think God works through doctors?" He encouraged us not to close ourselves off from logical thinking and put God to a foolish test. He reminded us that God had given the field of medicine the knowledge to heal.

The Defiant Ones

Our spiritual egos were so inflated, there was no way we were going to back down and agree with the doctor's position. Our rationale was simple. We believed God was on our side. Therefore, nothing and nobody was going to change our minds, not even a well-educated, experienced oncologist practicing in one of the major children's hospitals in America! Chris's unbelievable recovery from this devastating pneumonia was proof enough for us.

What Is Really Going on Here?

Then why didn't we feel real peace in our prayer time? Why did we struggle with doubt in our attempts to make a decision? Why did our defenses go up when we anticipated what Dr. Lee was going to say? Why did we lack strong conviction when we walked into his office? Why were we afraid of being wrong? Was God really on our side? Was it all about us versus them? Did we properly discern God's leading? A host of unanswered questions followed us into that crucial conference showdown.

Removing the Veil

As we listened to Dr. Lee, the light of God just went on in our hearts and minds. Suddenly, it all became very clear. The reason we had so many questions, doubts, and reservations about radiation was that we had not been listening to God. We tried to manufacture in our minds our desires and not God's. Why? Because we did not want to expose Chris to the side effects of radiation treatments. If God could heal her once, then why couldn't He do it again, right? Our prayers were selfish and wrong. We were trying to manipulate God. God gently used this wonderful, caring doctor to help us realize that we were wrong and that God's way was the right way. God was using and does use medicine in spectacular ways. Praise God for doctors and medical research!

A Lesson Learned

The important lesson we learned here was that true faith means trusting without a doubt the sovereignty of God. He knows what is best in all circumstances. God is always in control because He is always in the know. It's laying every fiber of your faith at the cross and being obedient to God's perfect, all-knowing will. This revelation would soon become a real turning point in my relationship with God in Christ.

Jan and I momentarily lost sight of the big spiritual picture. We had to come to a clearer understanding that we could count on God regardless of any trial. We needed to trust in God's supreme judgment and unconditional love in all situations. He knows what is best. Jesus said these profound encouraging words: "Which of you fathers, if your son asks for a fish, will give him a snake instead? Or if he asks for an egg, will give him a scorpion? If you then, though you are evil, know how to give good gifts to your children, how much more will your Father in Heaven give the Holy Spirit to those who ask Him?" (Luke 11:11–13).

Heart Condition

This passage speaks to the condition of the human heart. We are all flawed. There are times when we do things we should not do or when we think bad thoughts. Yet God still loves and cares for His children. If an imperfect father or mother operating in a corrupt world provides for his or her children, then how much more will God provide for and take care of His children! It is vital to recognize just how merciful and forgiving God is. God's desire is for every born-again believer in Christ to receive the awesome gift of His Holy Spirit. The Bible affirms that the wonderful, powerful, helping Holy Spirit is available to all believers in Christ. The Holy Spirit builds our character and empowers us to serve and grow in our faith. But we need to remember to *delight in the good things Jesus has done in our lives.*

The Fonz

Most of us remember the hit show back in the seventies called *Happy Days.* If you are too young to remember the show, you can catch the reruns on TV. *Happy Days* was by far Chris's favorite TV program. One of the main characters on the show was "the Fonz."

The Fonz was cool—so cool he would snap his fingers and the girls would come running to him. He could hit the jukebox with the side of his fist and the music would start playing. All of his peers hung on his every word. Without a doubt the Fonz epitomized what it meant to be cool.

In one of the episodes the Fonz was wrong about something. However, he could not bring himself to say the word *wrong*. How could the coolest guy admit he was wrong? That would have ruined his reputation for being cool!

Getting It Right

True humility is recognizing that we don't know it all. We don't have a lock on God's will for our lives. Spiritual humility is setting our pride aside and recognizing that we don't always have the answers. It's admitting that we can be wrong and be open to God's teaching and correction. The manner in which we came across to the doctor was like what my late father-in-law would jokingly say: "I once thought I was wrong, but I was mistaken." That had been our attitude for a season.

The lesson we learned back in Dr. Lee's office years ago still holds true for us today.

> Every day, Lord, I will lift up these three promises
> That I may keep You in my view.
> That my love for You will grow deeper.
> That I will remain close to You
> Each and every day.

If you have a bad day, ask Jesus to give you a better tomorrow.

"I Can See Clearly Now"
Words by: Johnny Nash
(Some lyrics paraphrased)

My vision is clear now the storm has passed.
I can see all the hindrances in my path,
All the darkness that impaired my way is gone
It's going to be a bright clear sunny day.

I know I'm going to see my way through; my hurting is over.
The rainbow is before me now.

Yes, it's going to be blue skies and sunshine surrounding
        me.
It's going to be a day filled with bright sunshine.

CHAPTER SEVEN

"I Can See Clearly Now"

Still Cruising

Life was good at this particular time in our lives. We were in a spiritual comfort zone. The hand of God was teaching, blessing, and ministering to us. The book of Joel affirmed God's intervention in our lives.

> Then the Lord will be jealous for His land and take pity on His people. The Lord will reply to them: I am sending you again, new wine and oil, enough to satisfy you fully; never again will I make you an object of scorn to the nations. I will drive the northern army far from you, pushing it into a parched and barren land, with its front columns going into the eastern sea and those in the rear into the western sea. And its stench will go up; its smell will rise. Surely He has done great things. Do not be afraid, O land; be glad and rejoice. Surely the Lord has done great things. (Joel 2:18-21)

Recharging and Restoring

God had honored Joel's faith. The Lord would answer his prayer, drive away an army of locusts, and restore the land. A bountiful harvest was on the way. There would be a tremendous outpouring of God's provision and blessings. However, there was a condition attached: the people would have to repent. God wants to bless all His people and honor sincere repentance from sin. This triggers His forgiveness and miraculous intervention. God can turn our pain, discouragement, frustrations, disappointments, and fears into victories and times of rejoicing. God has not only done great things in the past but will surely do great things in the present and in the future.

God was doing just that in our lives. He was restoring our spiritual batteries by building up our confidence. We were growing in our conviction that God would meet our deepest needs in Christ. God continued to assure us of His power and the promise of doing great things in our family's lives. His divine generator, the Holy Spirit, was transforming our human energy into Spiritual energy.

Can't Stop the Power

God's goodness was just overwhelming. We could not deny for a moment His presence. It seemed like Jesus was in everything we did. Jesus was there in our conversations, Jesus was there in my workplace, Jesus was there in our finances, Jesus was there in Chris's tests, and Jesus was there in Jan's prayer group. Lastly, Jesus was there when Chris, Connie, and Diane adjusted to the emotional and spiritual buzz that surrounded our family life. We were eating, thinking, sleeping, and drinking Jesus' teaching, truth, power, love, care, and forgiveness twenty-four seven!

Putting the Pieces Together

At the time, we did not see the big picture of God's intentions for our family. However, looking back years later left no doubt in my mind that God was putting His perfect plan and purpose in place for what was yet to come. As usual, God knew exactly what He was doing. God was slowly but intentionally putting together the pieces of the puzzle of coming events concerning Chris and the rest of our lives together.

We Were Going to Make It

As the song suggests, I can make it now because the storm is past, and all the negative things are gone. I have been praying for a rainbow and it has finally come. Yes, it's going to be a bright day filled with blue skies and sunshine. Our world at that time was filled with sunshine and blue skies. We were firmly convinced there wasn't any obstacle we could not overcome. We knew God was doing mighty wonderful things in our midst. Our spiritual fervor was founded on these OT verses: "Because of the Lord's great love we are not consumed, for His compassions never fail. They are new every morning; great is your faithfulness. I say to myself, the Lord is my portion; therefore I will wait for Him. The Lord is good to those whose hope is in Him, to the one who seeks Him" (Lamentations 3:22–25).

The prophet Jeremiah was buried in sorrow, sin, fear, and frustration. The people were in a very bad place. Jerusalem had fallen to the Babylonians, the temple was destroyed, and his heart was crushed. Many of the Jews had been slain and countless others taken into Babylonian captivity. Jeremiah cried because the nation was getting what it deserved. Society, in his day, was filled with corruption and spiritual decay. Through the trials and tribulations, Jeremiah saw a ray of hope in God. He trusted in God's grace and mercy. He remembered the faithfulness and goodness of God.

Steadfast Determination

Like Jeremiah, Jan and I were determined to build our lives around God's faithfulness, trusting that Jesus would respond to our daily needs. Our security was anchored in Jesus. Our hope for each day, week, month, and even Chris's next test was centered on God's unmoving love and compassion. We were stepping out in faith, determined to walk in the ways of Jesus every day, confident He would bless us. Peter shared these words: "But grow in the grace and knowledge of our Lord and Savior Jesus Christ. To Him be glory both now and forever" (2 Peter 3:18).

Notice Peter used two words every believer should focus on: *grace* and *knowledge*. Peter encourages every Christian to grow not only in the head knowledge of Jesus, but also in the grace of Jesus. It is so important that we use our intellect to understanding of spiritual things and apply its truths to our lives.

Radar Love

Jesus was on our radar screen. Jan and I realized we needed to continue growing in the grace and knowledge of Jesus every day. A traditional Christian hymn "What a Friend We Have in Jesus" said it all for us. The first two lines of this great hymn say, "What a friend we have in Jesus, All our sins and griefs to bear! What a privilege to carry everything to God in prayer." The more we grew in our faith, the more we realized our shortcomings. There was more room for growth. In facing the challenges surrounding Chris's illness, God was drawing us closer and closer to Jesus. He was preparing us to stand on His promises found in the Word. If we kept our eyes on Jesus, we could confront and deal with any problem that came our way. *With Jesus we find fullness; without Jesus we find emptiness.*

It Was a Very Good Year

The year 1975 and the first half of 1976 was a very good period for Chris as well as the rest of us. Her faith was growing by leaps and bounds. During this time she was in remission and not hospitalized. Occasionally Chris would have to undergo a bone marrow test and spinal injections to determine if she was still in remission. These bone marrow examinations were really hard on her. They were extremely painful and caused Chris intense emotional trauma. For one particular bone marrow test, Chris decided to put her trust in Jesus and asked Him to take the pain away during the procedure.

Faith Tested

James offered these profound encouraging words, "You want something but you do not get it. You kill and covet, but you cannot have what you want. You quarrel and fight. You do not have, because you do not ask God. When you ask, you do not receive, because you ask with wrong motives, that you may spend what you get on your pleasures" (James 4:2-3).

James words are challenging for sure. We live in a corrupt world. Throughout the pages of history the world has revolved around a "me, myself, and I" mentality. Human nature will fight, scratch, claw, and even destroy to satisfy our physical and emotional appetites. Peter was directing his attention toward believers, followers of Christ. We all have sinful tendencies to pray selfishly, for our own pleasures and desires. Occasionally, instead of seeking God's will in the matter, we pray for our wants and not for our needs. This kind of asking does not please or glorify the Lord. There is no question that our fallen natures can get us into trouble and distort God's purpose for our lives.

Asking for the Right Reasons

I believe there is nothing wrong with wanting to live without fear and pain. Chris did not pray or ask God to take her pain in a selfish manner. She was simply seeking Jesus' intervention to see her through this painful test. Matthew's gospel reads as follows:

Jesus went throughout Galilee, teaching in their synagogues, preaching the Good News of the Kingdom, and healing every disease and sickness among the people. News about Him spread all over Syria, and people brought to Him all who were ill with various diseases, those suffering severe pain, the demon-possessed, those having seizures, and the paralyzed, and He healed them. (Matthew 4:23–24)

Jesus preached to anyone who would listen, wherever they were. He preached on a central theme: the kingdom of God was right in front of them. Jesus proclaimed a God who cares and heals not only physically and emotionally but also spiritually. Chris put her faith into action and asked Jesus to do what He had already done in the Bible. She called upon the Lord to take away the pain of this bone marrow test. She stepped out in faith and trusted the Lord, and He delivered! Her childlike faith and Jesus' healing response in her previous bout with pneumonia and this bone marrow exam literally transformed her relationship with Jesus. As a little girl, Chris had learned an important life lesson: how to walk in her faith.

There Was No Pain

Yes, Jesus taking Chris's pain during this bone marrow test was absolutely huge for her and for us! Consider this: the procedure that day for the bone marrow test also included three spinals. The doctors would inject a bore needle about the size of a house nail into the crest of her pelvic bone to extract her bone marrow for the purpose of determining if her body was producing good cells. The oncology department at Children's Memorial Hospital prescribed this particular test on a regular basis to see if she was in remission. Praise the Lord, Chris could see clearly now, for her pain was gone and all the darkness of this very unpleasant procedure had disappeared!

How Sweet It Was

As I have mentioned, our faith was growing through various ministries. We were increasingly alert to God's presence and desires for us individually and as a family. Jesus' continual ministry to Chris gave us confirmation that God was in control. Connie and Diane were growing in their faith as well. Our evening family devotionals played a major role in our children's spiritual growth. Many of our negative feelings were being replaced with God's peace and power. Life was just sweet for us. There was such joy in our household that year. Up to that point it was the best year and a half we had experienced together. There was no question that God had been training, teaching, and building us up in the ways of faith for reasons yet to come.

A Time to Learn

God's blessings were flowing. Jan was experiencing dramatic encounters with Jesus Christ in her new spiritual rebirth. Chris, Connie, and Diane asked Jesus into their hearts. Our girls' salvation was a great relief and joy for both Jan and me. God's supernatural activity among us was exciting and undeniable. Joel wrote, "And afterward, I will pour out My Spirit on all people. Your sons and daughters will prophesy, your old men will dream dreams, your young men will see visions. Even on my servants, both men and women, I will pour out My Spirit in those days" (Joel 2:28-29).

Joel's prophecy of the Holy Spirit, recorded in the Old Testament, was also quoted by Peter in the New Testament in Acts 2:16-21. These prophetic signs and wonders spoken by Joel and Peter are available to all believers in Christ for all generations through the ages. Even during the last days, the mighty Holy Spirit of God with all His miraculous signs will be manifested in believers and the church. The outpouring of the Holy Spirit did not stop at Pentecost some two thousand years ago. I believe the Holy Spirit's power continues to pour out into believers today.

Like a Mighty Wind

Signs and wonders were being poured into us in ways we never dreamed possible. The Holy Spirit was sweeping through us like it did in the New Testament book of Acts. The Spirit was empowering, convicting, counseling, and calling us to serve. As a result, a sense of excitement, joy, and anticipation filled our hearts. The mighty wind of the Spirit engulfed Jan and me. We hungered for more of God's grace, peace, and strength, and the assurance of His presence every day. *To be filled with the Holy Spirit is to experience fullness in the Christian life.*

You Can't Put Out the Fire

The Holy Spirit left no doubt in our minds and hearts that God was real. We were on fire for the Lord! The Holy Spirit was strengthening our faith by the authority of Scripture. During this period we were introduced to Calvary Church in Naperville, Illinois. This growing church played a crucial role in our spiritual walk. We attended various conferences provided by Calvary's outreach ministries. These conferences were truly anointed by the Spirit of God, and energized our growing young faith.

Go and Serve

Our ministry opportunities were not restricted to attending Christian conferences. Jan's neighborhood prayer group was growing. God was moving not only numerically but also Spiritually among them. Physical healings were taking place for friends and family members, and others received Jesus as their Lord and

Savior. I served as a deacon in our home church. We also became active in Bible studies, Marriage Encounter, and women's and men's groups. Jan and I served as junior high advisers in our local church. Church ministries became the center of our lives, and we loved it. Who would have thought that I would become head-over-heels committed to the church? Yes, God is a God of miracles and surprises!

The In Crowd

Our inner circle of Christian friends became our lifeline. Some of the lyrics from this old Christian hymn speak not only to the importance of Christian fellowship, but also of just how crucial our Christian relationships were and are to us.

> Blest be the tie that binds—Our hearts in Christian love
> The fellowship of kindred minds—Is like to that above
> We share our mutual woes, We pour our ardent prayers
> And often for each other flows—The sympathizing tear
> From sorrow, toil, and pain—And sin, we shall be free
> And perfect love and friend-ship reign—Through eternity
> —The Reverend John Fawcett, 1782

Sharing and Caring

Luke wrote the following in the book of Acts:

All the believers were one in heart and mind. No one claimed that any of his possessions was his own, but they shared everything they had. With great power the apostles continued to testify to the resurrection of the Lord Jesus, and much grace was upon them all. There were no needy persons among them. For from time to time those who

owned lands or houses sold them, brought the money
from the sales and put it at the apostles feet, and it was
distributed to anyone as he had need. (Acts 4:32–35)

In these verses we find real Christian unity and action. There was
sincere Christian communion among those first believers. They prayed
together, and shared needs. The Holy Spirit today calls Christians
to exercise the same unity, compassion, and action. However, many
Christians today are not asked to sell their belongings or isolate themselves from society and establish communes. What is important is
loyalty, commitment, and love for brothers and sisters in Christ. We
are called to reach out and help those who need assistance, be it financial, physical, emotional, or whatever.

Sharing the Love

We were blessed with true, strong Christian fellowship that
was birthed by the revelations of God's Word. We shared a common bond with those of like spiritual minds. Our loyalty, sharing,
and caring was validated and solidified through the presence of the
Holy Spirit. We discovered that genuine biblical Christian friendship consists of two major elements. There must be a balance of
both a social and Spiritual interaction. What binds theses elements
together in Christian fellowship is living in a dynamic relationship
with Jesus Christ.

Our Christian friends became conduits for what was yet to come.
I will revisit how our Christian family played such an amazing role in
our lives in a later chapter. Allow me to close with this truth: *Where
there is Christian faith, Jesus' grace abounds.*

Facing adversity gives God an opportunity to exercise His supernatural ability.

"The Long and Winding Road"
Words by: Paul McCartney
(Some lyrics paraphrased)

The long and curving road always leads me to your door.
Through my tears and all the times I have tried and been
    alone.
All the things I have tried, yet I am always called back to the
    long and curving road.
A long time ago you left me standing by myself.
Don't let me stand there without you again.
Help me find a way back to you.

CHAPTER EIGHT

"The Long and Winding Road"

Preparing the Way

The long and curving road of Chris's battle with leukemia (I hate that ugly word) had been free of bumps for a while. However, that was about to change. During this relatively serene time, our cup was running over with the grace of God. God was building us up in the faith. You need to really understand the previous chapter. In it God was setting the foundation for our upcoming winding road. He was definitely preparing us spiritually. Time after time while on our winding road of events, we would cry out to Jesus and ask Him to wash away our pool of tears. Without fail He would lead us to the door of His love and mercy.

The Living Hope

Our faith was fueled by the living hope we had in Jesus. Second Peter says, "Praise be to the God and Father of our Lord Jesus Christ! In His great mercy He has given us new birth into a living hope through the resurrection of Jesus Christ from the dead, and into an inheritance that can never perish, spoil or fade-kept in Heaven for you" (2 Peter 1:3–4). Peter reminds us that we need to take salvation personally. As someone once so appropriately said, "If you were the only person on this earth, Jesus would have died on that cross just for you." When we trust and put our faith in Him, He gives us the greatest gift of all eternal life. We receive this new birth through the resurrection of Jesus. It doesn't get any better than this good news!

Refined by Fire

The power of Peter's words just burned within us. God was refining us with the mighty fire of His Holy Spirit.

> Who through faith are shielded by God's power until the coming of the salvation that is ready to be revealed in the last time. In this you greatly rejoice, though now for a little while you may have had to suffer grief in all kinds of trials. These have come so that your faith—of greater worth than gold, which perishes even though refined by fire—may be proved genuine and may result in praise, glory and honor when Jesus Christ is revealed. Though you have not seen Him, you love Him; and even though you do not see Him now, you believe in Him and are filled with an inexpressible and glorious joy, for you are receiving the goal of our faith, the salvation of your souls. (1 Peter 1:5-9)

God's deliverance is followed by our steady perseverance.

Cashing In on the Blessings

During this calm year and a half, we were learning the basic fundamentals of the faith. These verses from First Peter gave us encouragement in the good times, and would also give us encouragement and strength when confronting the coming trials. God knew we were going to be facing music we did not want to hear. He was preparing our faith for what was to come. He was teaching us the basic fundamentals of the Christian walk. God was refining us as we grew closer and closer to Jesus. The Holy Spirit was revealing to us many biblical nuggets. His blessings were being poured out on us from all directions.

Wonderful Moments

We felt the glow and wonder of Jesus' love. God was drawing our family together in Christian unity. Listening to our girls' prayer requests during evening devotionals was beautiful and heartwarming. Connie's and Diane's prayers for their sister's health would have melted even the most hardened heart. How rewarding it was to watch our girls' faith grow by leaps and bounds!

Keeping the Main Thing the Main Thing

Children's Memorial Hospital's social services department had given us a sobering statistic about families trying to cope with a terminally ill child. Approximately 50 percent of the marriages fail. However, Jan and I were growing stronger in our marital relationship because we anchored our marriage in Jesus and the promises of Scripture.

We were seeking to live our lives and raise our children in ways that would please the Lord. Our goal was to keep our eyes fixed on Jesus and to live our lives the way He wanted us to live and teach these truths to our children. Without a doubt we occasionally fell short. But God was gracious and patient as we pressed on in obedience. The following truth was our driving force in those days: *pointing our lives in God's direction is to tap into His perfection.*

A Storm Was Brewing

Although Chris was still in remission, her lab counts began revealing some strange results, which perplexed even the doctors. What was going on? Why couldn't they give us some medical answers to these irregularities? We didn't know what was going on and the scary part was that the doctors didn't either, but we kept the faith. In First John we read, "There is no fear in love. But perfect love drives out fear" (1 John 4:18). God demonstrated His perfect love for us on the cross. John reminds all believers that God wants us to trust and follow Him because of His love for us. Therefore, we overcome our fears by focusing on God's unconditional love. We need to recognize as born-again Christians that it is only by Jesus' mercy and love that we have the capacity to overcome trials of the flesh.

Jesus, Our Pilot

The knowledge of our new birth in Jesus was being put to the test. We could either relinquish to the flesh or trust and obey Christ. Paul penned these encouraging words: "You have been set free from sin, and become slaves to righteousness" (Romans 6:18). Paul tells us that before Christ, we were controlled by the old nature and were slaves to sin and corruption. Now that we have received Christ, we follow a new master, who sets us free from sin. Jan and I had enough wisdom to understand that Jesus had given us a second chance. We had experienced a complete do-over in Jesus. We placed our fears at the foot of the cross. We knew something was up, and the wind of the storm was starting to gust.

Let's Go Camping

In the summer of '76 we went to Timberlee, a Christian camp in Wisconsin, with my brother Steve, his wife, Sharon, and their four children. Chris, Connie, and Diane were really excited to go on this week of camping. They liked hanging out with their cousins Vicky, Rick, Jeannie, and Mike. Chris particularly looked up to her older cousin Vicky. All was well in Chris's world when Vicky was around.

Chris smiled a lot on that camping trip. The week at Timberlee was a good diversion for Chris, even though we had to take her back to the hospital for blood tests. It was also a pleasant change of pace for Jan and me. We enjoyed the camp teachings and company of my brother and his family.

The Gift That Keeps on Giving

At Camp Timberlee we began to experience more of God's manifestations. Paul wrote,

> Now to each one the manifestation of the Spirit is given for the common good. To one there is given through the Spirit the message of wisdom, to another the message of knowledge by means of the same Spirit, to another faith by the same Spirit, to another gifts of healing by that one Spirit, to another miraculous power, to another prophecy, to another distinguishing between spirits, to another speaking in different kinds of tongues, and to still another the interpretation of tongues. All these are the work of one and the same Spirit, and He gives them to each one, just as He determines. (1 Corinthians 12:7-11)

Paul lists the Spiritual gifts given to believers for building up the body. These particular gifts of the Spirit are not given to believers based on their natural abilities or talents. Paul reminds us that every Christian has at least one Spiritual gift.

Why Can't We All Get Along?

Now, there have been huge disagreements among Christians about the miraculous (charismatic) gifts of the Holy Spirit. Strong theological differences over some of these spectacular Spiritual gifts have divided churches and its members for centuries. Some denominations, theologians, and Christians in the pew believe that not all of the Spiritual gifts were meant to be permanent. They argue that some of these so-called spectacular gifts are not necessary for the modern church, because we now have the full revelation of God's Word, the Bible.

The Battle Lines Are Drawn

I believe Satan has used this Spiritual gift debate to create division within the body of Christ, called the church. The purpose for writing this book is not to promote a particular theological agenda. This book is not about affirming any particular denominational, theological, or doctrinal point of view concerning the gifts of the Spirit. I am simply sharing how God showed up in the events that took place in the lives of an average and at times, very unassuming family. We were a family that was desperately reaching out to God in Christ with a terminally ill child. During this time God manifested Himself to us in supernatural ways. By no means will I ever apologize for that, for to do so would be to deny all the signs and wonders God had shown us through the awesome power of His mighty Holy Spirit.

I'm Just Saying

I am merely reporting how we lived and experienced the power of God throughout our ordeal. The reader can draw his or her own theological conclusions. We can debate who is right and who is wrong, but our story is centered on Jesus' intervention and not on advocating a certain theological preference. What is of utmost importance in our story is for Jesus Christ to be honored and glorified.

Putting It into Perspective

Paul put it all in perspective when he said, "Therefore, as it is written, let him who boasts boast in the Lord" (1 Corinthians 1:31). I am in total agreement with the apostle Paul. Jesus is all that you and I will ever need. He is our trusted redeemer; our grace; our helper; our strength; our comforter; our closest, most dependable friend; our wisdom; our righteousness; our Lord and Savior—all that we will ever need! Therefore, *"Let him who boasts boast in the Lord."* AMEN!

The Ultimate Question

I believe the ultimate two-part question we must address in life is who is Jesus, and what do you do with Him? The Bible tells us Jesus is at the very center of life. He is both God and man, meaning He is fully God and fully human simultaneously. He died in place of our sins. By faith we receive His grace of eternal life, and His Holy Spirit gives us the power, truth, conviction, and knowledge of the Word, to know and do His will. This is Christianity 101, "the nuts and bolts" of the faith. The Bible reminds us from time to time of the importance for every believer to brush up on the basics of the faith. "Only let us live up to what we have already attained" (Philippians 3:16).

No Restrictions

Allow me to present a word of caution. Since God in Christ created this whole world, raised the dead, healed the sick, cast out demons, and much more, doesn't it make sense that He is capable of doing anything He chooses to do, with whomever, whenever, wherever, and whatever? My point is that He is sovereign over all things, even the use of all the spiritual gifts as recorded in the Bible. Absolutely nothing is beyond God's reach. Jesus confirmed this in Mark: "If you can'? said Jesus. Everything is possible for him who believes" (Mark 9:23). Yes, there are times when God sends us love letters even in our darkest hours. The song "Love Letters," written by Diana Krall, attests to this truth.

Here is a paraphrased version.

There may not be a star shining in a moonless night.

But I believe deep within my heart you love me, because you said you did.

Those love letters I received have come directly from our heart and they draw us closer

Even when we are separated.

I know that I am not alone because of the love letters you write.

I have memorized each and every word and I read them over and over again.

For I know every line comes from within your heart.

Divine Love Letters

While at Camp Timberlee, Jan began receiving revelations from God. She would enter them in her journal. Now, you can call her messages from God prophecies, words of knowledge, or whatever, but for the sake of argument, I'll call them love letters straight from God's heart to Jan's heart. Jeremiah said, "Call to me and I will answer you and tell you great unsearchable things you do not know" (Jeremiah 33:3). God offered this great assurance to Jeremiah: all he had to do was call out to the Lord. God would respond and reveal truths that only He (God) could know. Jan petitioned God in prayer many times during this period in our lives. God would also fill her heart with knowledge of events to come that only He could possibly know. She humbled herself before the Lord and trusted that God would acknowledge her prayers and that what He revealed to her would come to pass. She simply reached out to the God of Abraham, Isaac, and Jacob and believed that all things are possible with the Almighty God.

A Divine Secret

One day at Camp Timberlee, God sent Jan a love letter. God's love letter said this: Chris would have a new birth, Jan would have another baby, his name would be David, and Chris and I would choose the name for confirmation. She later talked to Chris about the new addition to the family but did not reveal the baby's name. The last part of the love letter included the following: I would have a new job, a financial change would take place, and we would have a new home. Jan recorded all seven events in her journal but kept this love letter a secret until God appointed the right time for it to be revealed.

Sharing the News

Several months later Jan shared the news of her pregnancy with Chris. Chris was excited that she and her sisters were going to have a baby brother. At that time Jan told Chris that Dad would confirm the baby's name. A month or so later, the whole family was gathered around the supper table. We began talking about possible names for our coming new addition. I picked the name David Joseph, which was the same name God had given Chris and Jan separately! Chris jumped with joy when I chose the name David. Friends, is God awesome or what? The other parts of God's "love letter" were yet to come.

What Is Going On?

Our camping trip was behind us. Chris developed strange hot spots on her hands and feet. The doctors were suspicious and knew that something was not right. She was still in remission, but there was a heightened concern about her medical condition.

A Time of Anxiety

We were in the realm of the unknown, as though we were stuck in some kind of twilight zone. However, through it all we knew God was in control. We started to experience some anxiety and concern about the direction of Chris's health. Chris was experiencing more and more physical discomfort. Jan and Chris spent more time traveling back and forth to the hospital for tests. I was working most of the time. Jan and Chris grew very close as mother and daughter. It was amazing to see the spiritual strength that Jan modeled not only in Chris's life, but also for Connie, Diane, and me. My time would come later.

By Christmas of '76, Chris's blood counts were so bad that she had to spend a few days at Children's Memorial Hospital for blood transfusions. There was growing concern about her condition. The doctors were baffled and not sure what was going on. Chris was now ten years old and had grown accustomed to the hospital environment. She developed strong friendships with other children suffering from leukemia and other terminal diseases.

A Little Friend Remembered

One of Chris's friends at Children's was Billy. Billy had leukemia and became special to Chris, Jan and myself. He had this contagious, outgoing personality. When Billy walked into a room, everybody seemed to take notice. He was a handsome little seven-year-old with huge brown eyes and possessed a wonderful, joyful view of life. Billy lived his young life with zest.

The Sad News

The hospital pretty much let the kids roam around the oncology floor. They wanted the children to feel as comfortable and at home as possible. On a few occasions when Chris was in the hospital, Billy was also there. One evening while I was resting in one of the lounges, Billy showed up with his usual smile and introduced me to the stuffed animal he carried with him wherever he went. Billy told me all about his little friend and then went on his way. On one occasion Billy shared with Jan his concern about his mother. He was afraid his mommy would feel sad when he died. Billy's fear and concern for his mother proved just how special these children with terminal illnesses really and truly are. A time came when we noticed that Billy had not been at the clinic for his check-ups. We inquired and were told that Billy had passed away. It was a hard day for all of us. I will never forget that enthusiastic, upbeat, brown-eyed boy who, in such a brief period of time, captured my heart.

A Time for Everything

The book of Ecclesiastes reads, "There is a time for everything, and a season for every activity under Heaven: A time to be born and a time to die a time to plant a time to uproot" (Ecclesiastes 3:1–2).

The writer reminds us that there is a time for everything. As Christians it is important to find peace and accept God's timing, even when death strikes a family member or friends. It is true that the loss of a child hits us the hardest, because it just isn't natural for the young to die. We expect children to grow up and live full lives. We cannot always explain why God does what He does. But one thing is sure and true: He always knows what is best. We need to trust that we can call on God for comfort, strength, and peace in a time of tragedy, pain, and loss. We need to enjoy the moments of life that God has so richly given us. I understand there are times when this is very hard to do. However, there is no substitute for Jesus' loving, caring presence in times of suffering and heartache. Yes, we can call out to Jesus, for He will never leave us alone as we travel on our "long and winding road." We just need to remember this good news: *Jesus is in control when you give Him your heart, mind and soul.*

God doesn't want us to wait for our afflictions to strike before we turn to Him. He wants us to turn our hearts and minds to Him at this very moment.

"I'll Be There"
Words by: Berry Gordy, Bob West, Hal Davis and Willie
    Hutch
(Some lyrics paraphrased)

Let us make a vow that love will bind us together.
I will reach for you and trust in everything you do.
Just call me and there I will be.

It is there that you will find comfort.
My world with its hopes and dreams will be centered on
    you.
I am so happy you have come into my life.

The power of love will be your strength.
Yes, I will grab hold of you.
All I want to do is make your life filled with joyous
    laughter.
Just call to me and I will come into your presence.

I will be your protection; my unconditional love for you is
    filled with my adoration.
I will always be there for you whenever you call out to me.
If there would come a time when you discover someone else,
He had better treat you well. If that doesn't happen,
I'll be waiting.

CHAPTER NINE

"I'll Be There"

The Beginning of the End

Chris's blood transfusions were becoming more frequent. She spent an increased amount of time at Children's Memorial Hospital. The doctors still could not give us concrete medical reasons for her deteriorating condition. Jan and I were gripped with fear and uncertainty. It was hard to hide our concerns from Chris and her little sisters.

The severity of her health issues carried with it a serious atmospheric mood swing that started to create some uneasiness in Connie and Diane. Later on in this chapter, I share what Connie and Diane felt during this intense period. The only comment I will make at this time is that my daughters were and still are two very special heroes in my life. They went through, and rose above, a ton of adversity at young and innocent ages. The hand of God was truly on them throughout this ordeal.

Thrown a Life Preserver

The song "I'll Be There" really speaks to the most trying time I have ever spent on this side of heaven. We were clinging to God by our fingernails. It's safe to say that *panic* is the word that most accurately describes our emotions and actions at the time. In the book of Proverbs we read, "Trust in the Lord with all your heart and lean not on your own understanding; In all your ways acknowledge Him, and He will keep your paths straight" (Proverbs 3:5-6).

The writer was not suggesting that we become brain dead when facing difficult choices. God has blessed us with the ability to think, reason, and come to logical conclusions. We are not simply called to be a bunch of Spocks. Instead the writer of Proverbs is encouraging us to lift up our decisions before God and ask for His wisdom and guidance in all matters. There was no question that our lives were in turmoil. It felt like we were going down for the third time. Then at just the right time God would throw us another divine life preserver. Nobody on this planet seemed to know what was going on with Chris, except God. In our dazed and confused state, we reached out in trust and sought to be obedient to our Lord Jesus. God was always faithful and in His infinite wisdom knew what we needed at the right time. He was always there.

Was She Strong?

The paraphrased version of the song says I will reach for you and trust everything you do. Just call me, and there I will be. As I mentioned earlier, things were getting extremely stressful. Chris was at Children's Memorial Hospital more than she was home. She had an unbelievable will and determination to fight this ugly and cruel disease. During the Christmas holidays she had to have another blood transfusion. Chris tried to be upbeat, but she was incredibly tired and her energy level was extremely low. It was often a challenge to solicit even a smile from her. Jan would say, "Chris, how about a smile?" and it would take most of her energy to muster a weak grin. But she never felt sorry for herself. Not once did I ever hear her complain and say, "This isn't fair; why did I have to get this disease? Why do I have to go through all this pain and discomfort?" Through it all, Chris reached out to receive her Lord's hand, with a simple yet profound faith. She could call on the name of her Lord Jesus, and He would be there.

What Could Happen Next?

On top of our upheaval, Jan was in the last trimester of her pregnancy and developed a blood clot in her right leg. She used a wheelchair for the remainder of her pregnancy. Her doctor would not allow her to be on her feet more than ten minutes at a time.

Christians Rise to the Occasion

Many of our church family and friends pitched in and drove Jan to the hospital in Chicago, where I would pick her up after work. Once again God's hand was in all the details. God blessed us with wonderful godly friends. Ken and Carol Seidel were a blessing from heaven. Their three little girls were our daughters' best friends. With our frequent trips to Children's, Ken and Carol embraced Connie and Diane, loving and caring for them like they were their own. We will never forget their acts of kindness, love, and support to our girls at a time in their lives when they desperately needed it.

Moving On

As we moved into mid-January of '77, our lives appeared to be as bleak as the Midwest's winter weather. It seemed as though our frustration level was being pushed to the limit. The concern for Jan's blood clot, coupled with Chris's deteriorating condition with no medical answers, filled my heart with pain and anxiety. Jesus said, "Ask and it will be given to you; seek, and you will find; knock and the door will be opened to you. For everyone who asks receives; he who seeks finds; and to him who knocks, the door will be opened" (Matthew 7:7–8). Jesus knows all of us will feel the heat in the course of living life. The hits come, and some will bring us to our knees. When they come—and make no mistake, they will come—it often becomes difficult to reach out and obey His Word and trust that He is in control. But Jesus reminds us that if we are to find strength, true peace, guidance, comfort, and hope in times of strife, we must keep asking Him. He wants us to be persistent and keep knocking at the door of His goodness, to seek His strength, wisdom, and compassion. Then He will supply all the grace that is necessary in every situation to press on and be victorious. It is crucial to understand that *God can turn our setbacks into supernatural comebacks.*

Lord, This Is Getting Really Tough

My stomach was in knots, but Jan and I kept knocking, asking, seeking, and praying to the Lord. By no means were our prayers meek and halfhearted. We knew deep within that God would respond to our cries for help. Therefore, it never crossed our minds to just give up and throw in the towel. There was no turning back as far as we were concerned. The idea of bailing out and giving up on God wasn't even an option for us. He had taken care of us up to this point. Regardless of how increasingly ugly it would get, our prayer requests became more sincere and intense. *In order to follow God's way, we must learn to pray.*

Then It Happened

At the end of January 1977, Chris had a major seizure at home and had to be taken by ambulance to intensive care at Children's Memorial Hospital. Her fever reached an unprecedented 106 degrees. She slowly regained some strength and spent all of February in the hospital. Chris was never quite the same after running such a high temperature. She was glad to receive hundreds of valentines from her fifth-grade classmates as well as from other classes at her school. Chris was now so weak that she could not send valentines back to school on her own, so Jan had to help her.

Could It Get Any Worse?

The doctors contemplated surgery on a cyst that had developed behind Chris's right knee. She had not walked for a month because of a general lack of strength, the cyst, and a series of blood transfusions. Jan's blood clot prevented her from walking. In fact, she had not walked for a month herself. She could not drive or stand during this time that Chris was in the hospital. She was restricted to a wheelchair with one leg elevated.

Denny Pouts

I was in a really bad place coming home from the hospital after one of those long, trying nights. Chris was trying hard to be well, but her concentration and strength were not there. She was clearly losing ground. I was in a nasty mood, angry, frustrated, scared, and confused about what was going on. We settled Connie and Diane down and put them to bed. Jan and I proceeded to our bedroom and I vented. I basically said, "What is going on here? Chris is not getting any better; it's just one thing after another. On top of Chris's serious issues, you're struggling with this blood clot. We—I—need to know if God is in this. Where is God? Where is Jesus? We've got to know if He is still in control of this mess. We need some signs from Jesus now!"

SOS Time

In some ways I felt like Job in the Bible. It was SOS time for me. I wanted to know what Jesus was up to. I wanted to know if Jesus would be there with a love so strong that it could not be denied. I yearned for Jesus' presence. I hungered for Him to keep holding on to us. I did not want Him to let go for even a second. "Please, sweet Jesus, help," I pleaded. "Please, Jesus, hold us up. Please, Jesus, don't let us down!" I humbled myself before the Lord, with a hurting and broken heart. I did so without any reservation or embarrassment.

It was breaking my heart seeing the worry on my pregnant wife's face, her inability to function in the way she wanted to on behalf of her dying daughter. I am not making excuses here to justify my actions. I was vulnerable. I was losing control. I needed help and needed it fast, and I needed it right then. So I cried out to the Lord for His mercy and grace.

Traveling Light with Jesus

Jesus said and taught many profound things, but I want us to look at this one closely. Jesus said, "Come to Me, all you who are weary and burdened, and I will give you rest. Take My yoke upon you and learn from Me, for I am gentle and humble in heart, and you will find rest for your souls. For my yoke is easy and My burden is light" (Matthew 11:28-30). There are times when we just don't get it. We don't have a clue what God is up to, and our frustration shows up clearly on our emotional radar screen. This is especially true in those moments when we ask, what more can I do? Friends, it is at this fork in the road of our lives that Jesus invites us to come to Him for support and receive a holy power the world cannot give. I believe that is exactly what Jesus was saying in this passage. Jesus wants to set us free from our heavy burdens. Jesus offers us His lifesaving yoke. Our growing in the faith is predicated on understanding that Jesus provides rest and welcomes all those who humbly come to Him and believe His yoke is easy and His burden is light.

In Our Room

That night in our bedroom I dumped all my baggage on Jesus and held nothing back. Not only did I want to, but I also believed it was Jesus' will to free Jan and myself from our heavy burdens. We came to the cross with a raw, uninhibited trust in our Master. I believed if we called on Jesus, He would show up. The doctors at Children's were just wonderful. How blessed we were to have the gift of doctors. God truly uses them in countless wonderful ways. Because of research and the brilliance of those in the health professions, we are living longer and enjoying better-quality lives. We also recognize that doctors don't possess all knowledge. In Chris's case they were stumped. Like the rest of us, doctors are finite, so we turned to the infinite God for answers, to lighten our load.

Can You Believe It?

I turned to Jan and said, "Let's pray and ask God to give us some hope, affirmation and signs that He is in control of all the crazy, mysterious events surrounding Chris's current medical condition. Let's ask God to reveal His presence through Scripture so we can have some kind of assurance that His hand is guiding this catastrophe." We began praying separately in silence, seeking the yoke of Christ to lighten our burden. After a brief time of silent prayer, without uttering a word, Jan opened her Bible. Keep in mind, she was on the other side of the bed so I could not see what Scripture she was reading. I continued in prayer, petitioning our Lord. Then He laid a Scripture passage on my heart. When I asked Jan for the passage God had given her, what she shared just blew me away. God had given me the same Scripture! We were in shock and awe. What were the odds that we would receive the same book, chapter, and verses without conferring with each other? How is that for confirmation? Glory to God: Jesus was in control! What a huge boost this was to our faith. The assurance of Jesus' presence welled up inside of us. His goodness and mercy prevailed. We called out His name and He was there. Later on, this supernatural manifestation occurred a second time in our prayer time together.

Home for the Last Time

Chris was able to come home for the first two weeks in March of 1977. What a special time it was for both Jan and me (Connie and Diane do not remember Chris being home for those two weeks). During this time, Chris slept with Jan in our king-sized bed because it was difficult for both of them to sleep at night. Since I had to get up early for work, we decided it would be best if I slept in another room. This was really good for Jan to be able to spend extra time with Chris, especially in light of what was to come. Chris and Jan treated their nights together like an ongoing slumber party. Both were up at all hours of the night snacking on Twinkies and peanut butter cookies. They were just having fun hanging out together.

Our Church Family

In a later chapter I pay tribute to all those wonderful people at Fox Valley Presbyterian Church in Geneva and our other friends who lovingly and graciously carried part of the load for us in so many ways. Words cannot adequately express what their ministries meant to our family and what they still mean to us today. During Chris's thirty-day stay in the hospital we had thirty meals brought into our home while we were driving back and forth. What a wonderful group of people we had holding us up.

Love Is the Answer

Jesus said, "A new command I give you: Love one another. As I have loved you, so you must love one another. By this all men will know that you are my disciples, if you love one another" (John 13:34–35). Jesus challenges us to take and apply love at the highest level. We are to love our brothers, sisters, friends, and neighbors as Jesus loved us. How much did Jesus love us? We find the answer in Jesus' words from John 15:13: "Greater love has no one than this; that he lay down his life for his friends." Jesus called His disciples friends. His death on the cross was proof of just how much He loved them. Now Jesus commanded His disciples, and He commands us, to prove our love for Him by loving others. Therefore, we are to love each other as Jesus loved us. It was a love so great that He was willing to sacrifice His life for us. As Jesus loves us, we are called in turn to proclaim and model His unconditional love to others.

Chrissy's Girls

Chris's love for her sisters, Connie and Diane, grew as her faith grew. During her February stay in the hospital, we would wheel her down to the gift shop so she could buy gifts, stuffed animals, and such for her sisters. When we visited Chris, the first thing on her agenda was to hear about Connie and Diane. She wanted a blow-by-blow account of everything they were up to. She loved and missed them so much.

Home Away from Home

Chris's seizure had a traumatic effect on Connie and Diane. Jan and I were preoccupied with Chris's medical concerns, yet we wanted to make sure we made the necessary arrangements for Connie's and Diane's care and emotional well-being. Once again Ken and Carol Seidel came through, not only for us but also for Connie and Diane.

Outside of our home, the Seidel household was the next best option for them. Earlier in Chris's illness, we asked Connie and Diane who they would like to stay with when Mommy and Daddy had to spend so much time with Chris in the hospital. Without hesitation they said it was the Seidels. It really helped that our children's best friends just happened to be Ken and Carol's little girls Michelle and Heather. How is that for God's provision? This was by no means an indict-ment against the many other friends who were there for the girls. We deeply appreciated their love and care also.

True Friends

Our hearts went out to Ken and Carol's oldest daughter, Nancy, Chris's best friend. How difficult this whole mess was for her. Nancy and Chris were alike in many ways. They shared common interests and did all sorts of crafts together. Nancy was very aware of Chris's physical limitations. However, Chris's deficiencies never hindered their close friendship. Some of Chris's friends backed away from her because of her illness, but Nancy was always there for her. All of us who have developed true friendships based on unconditional love like that between Nancy and Chris have been blessed.

Connie and Diane Remember

I recently asked Connie and Diane to express as best they could how they felt in Chris's final days. It was emotionally overwhelming to hear them express the pain, sorrow, heartache, and confusion they experienced at such young and innocent ages. Their words caused Jan and me to weep for them once again. We were so caught up in what Chris was going through, we never fully realized the depth of Connie's and Diane's pain at such a critical time.

The following is a summary of what Connie was feeling as she approached her eighth birthday. After Chris's seizure, she knew

Chris was going to die. Connie was aware that Chris would not get better and was afraid she would never see her again. She wondered why we would wake her up when we returned from the hospital with stuffed animals that Chris wanted to give them. Connie said she did not know how to react, so she did not talk about it and kept everything inside. She didn't want Mom and Dad to know her feelings, and thought she had to be strong for Mom and Dad. Connie was comfortable spending time at the Seidels; she felt they were loved and wanted there. Connie said the Seidel house was like their second home. She thought of Carol as her surrogate mother. Connie concluded by saying that she knew Chris was "really sick" and would not get better.

Here are Diane's own words in describing her thoughts about Chrissy in her last weeks.

> The last months before Chrissy died seemed so long. I can remember longing to see her and talk with her, and hoping I would get that chance. My parents, one night after being at the hospital with Chrissy, brought Connie and me stuffed animals that Chrissy had picked out for us. That was very important to me. I really wanted to know the details behind the purchase: Did Chrissy actually pick them out, or did you guys, Mom and Dad? What did she say as she was picking them out for me . . . about me? What did she say about me? I really needed to know, was she thinking about me and missing me the way I was thinking about and missing her?

> I can also recall just knowing she was going to die. I can remember talking to Mom and Dad and asking them what I knew the answer to: "Is Chrissy going to die?" My dad responded, "No, no, no, she is going to get better, sweetie." I knew in my heart she was going to die, so this made me

feel sad, and I had heartache for my mom and dad because I was worried about how they were going to take it when she did die.

When I went to school, I hoped no one would bring up anything about Chrissy. It was important to me for some reason that I not cry at school about this. I just wanted to appear as if everything was fine, although it was not. Maybe it was because at school, I could pretend everything was fine.

When you read the Bible and pray, the Holy Spirit will guide your day.

"Lean on Me"
Words by: Bill Withers
(Some lyrics paraphrased)

There are times in our lives when we experience pain and grief.
Just hold on to me when you feel weak and I will be there for you.
I will help you make it through.

A time will come when I will need to call on someone to give me support.
If there is a burden too heavy for you to carry
I will be there to help you carry that burden.

Brother, whenever you need a helping hand, remember you can always count on me.
So just give me a call.

Because there will surely come a time
When I will need a helping hand from someone.

CHAPTER TEN

"Lean on Me"

Come, Let's Reason Together

On March 15, 1977, Chris began having breathing problems and I took her to the hospital. They admitted her, thinking she had pneumonia. In the meantime Jan's neighborhood prayer group started ratcheting up the prayers not only for Chris's increased health problems, but also for Jan's health. Jan's due date was only a couple of weeks away. She was advised by doctors and friends not to spend so much time at Children's. Jan hated the thought of being away from Chris. She fought the idea of not spending nights at the hospital. We worked out a compromise: Jan would visit during the day and go home at night. On the positive side, this brief arrangement gave her an opportunity to spend good-quality time with Connie and Diane.

Somebody to Lean On

I admitted Chris, and the doctors scheduled some preliminary tests. The tests revealed that Chris was still in remission without a trace of pneumonia. I thought, what is going on here? Once again we were faced with many questions but no answers. It was becoming very evident that Chris was losing ground. However, her faith remained incredibly strong. Throughout this whole ordeal Chris leaned on her Lord.

The Why Questions

Perhaps the million-dollar question for most of us when afflic-tion comes our way is Why the pain and heartache? Chris never complained about her plight. Her concerns weren't common for a child her age. Chris's world was not centered on birthday parties, attending summer camps, inviting her classmates over for fun, or going to movies. No, her world was centered on the next painful test, the next transfusion, the next bone marrow test, the next spi-nal, the next finger prick, the next IV, the next doctor probing her little body. I just praise the Lord for lifting Chris above her horrible circumstances. She truly depended on Jesus every day. *Trusting Jesus day by day prevents our fears from getting in the way.*

Somewhere Over the Rainbow

One stormy day while driving home on the Eisenhower Expressway after visiting Chris, I was in deep sorrow and heavily burdened. I started praying, seeking the Lord's comfort. I asked God to give me an extra touch of His grace. As I lifted up my petitions to the Lord, right in front of me, stretched across the sky, appeared this awesome rainbow. My faith was on shaky ground. I looked to the Lord for con-firmation of His presence, and lo and behold He came through once again! He knew precisely what I needed. He gave me the sign of the rainbow.

In the book of Genesis, God made a covenant with Noah.

> Then God said to Noah and to his sons with him: I now establish My covenant with you and with your descendents after you and with every living creature that was with you—the birds, the livestock and all the wild animals, all those that came out of the ark with you—every living creature on earth. I establish my covenant with you: Never

again will all life be cut off by waters of a flood; never again will there be a flood to destroy the earth. And God said, This is a sign of the covenant I am making between me and you and every living creature with you, a covenant for all generations to come: I have set my rainbow in the clouds, and it will be the sign of the covenant between me and the earth. Whenever I bring clouds over the earth and the rainbow appears in the clouds, I will remember my covenant between Me and you and all living creatures of every kind. Never again will the waters become a flood to destroy all life. Whenever the rainbow appears in the clouds, I will see it and remember the everlasting covenant between God and all living creatures of every kind on earth. So God said to Noah, this is the sign of the covenant I have established between Me and all life on the earth. (Genesis 9:8–17)

Divine Promise Keeper

God made a covenant (agreement) not only with Noah but with all humankind. In this covenant God made three distinct promises: 1) never again would a flood destroy all life; 2) never again would a flood destroy the earth; and 3) whenever the rainbow appears, it will be a reminder or a sign of God's covenant promise to humanity between Him and His creation. The rainbow is a reminder of God's loving faithfulness. Before there can be a rainbow, there must be a storm. In my rainbow God gave me a sign. He is faithful even in the midst of the great storm and dark clouds covering our battered lives. No matter what happened, nothing would separate us from God's love in Christ Jesus. Once again God gave me the sign of hope and belief. I could go on for another second, another minute, another hour, another day, another week, another month, as long as Jesus was guiding, encouraging, and comforting me.

"Just Remember I Love You"
Words by: Rick Roberts
(Some lyrics paraphrased)

When life gets chaotic,
The rainy days come and the nights seemed endless.

When you reach a point that you feel like you were born
    to fail.
When your troubles overwhelm you and you just want to
    cry out in frustration.
When the world around you seems to be falling apart.
And things just don't make sense to you.
When your plans have diminished and your dreams have
    left you
Wondering and your friends have disappointed you,
Just keep in mind that my love for you will make things right.
I want you to understand I love you more than I can put
    into words.

These paraphrased words from the song by Firefall all bring back memories of the rainbow I saw on that expressway years ago. I asked for a sign from God. I hungered for His presence, I hungered to know He was there, I hungered for a fresh dose of His promises. God responded by sending the rainbow, symbolizing His covenant: "Denny, I will always be there for you and everything will work out in its own time. Remember, my love for you goes beyond words." God's love touched my heart in a powerful way, more than I could ever express when I saw that rainbow. Thank you, Jesus, thank you, Lord, for hearing my plea! I love you so much. You are truly my One and only!

Lord, Did We Hear You Correctly?

When God placed His "love letter" (mentioned in chapter 8) on Jan's heart, months earlier at Camp Timberlee, we rejoiced, because one of the seven things that would come to pass was that Chris would have a new birth. Well, we just assumed that meant God was going to heal her from leukemia. I must be honest: that is what we wanted to hear. After all did not Jesus say, "They will pick up snakes with their hands; and when they drink deadly poison, it will not hurt them at all; they will place their hands on sick people, and they will get well" (Mark 16:18)? There is no question in my mind that the Scriptures affirm that God performs miracles and can heal and protect His followers today. After all, that is what He had done for His disciples in this passage and Chris's pneumonia months earlier. So it just made sense to us to expect another miracle.

God's Healing Hand

The book of James reminds us in chapter 5:14-15, "Is any one of you sick? He should call the elders of the church to pray over him and anoint him with oil in the name of the Lord. And the prayer offered in faith will make the sick person well; the Lord will raise him up. If he has sinned he will be forgiven." James was saying that if anyone is sick, the church leaders should anoint that person with oil (a symbol of the Spirit) and pray for a physical or spiritual healing. God can and does heal miraculously. Even some of the doctors at Children's Memorial Hospital could not deny that Chris had experienced a miraculous intervention when she'd had pneumonia. It is also true that not everyone will be healed. This fact should not discourage Christians from confessing their sins and praying for each other. Back then, I wasn't thinking about putting my hand in a rattlesnake pit or drinking deadly poison. However, I firmly believed it was not out of the realm of possibility that Chris's new birth would be a healing miracle.

Keeping Hope Alive

We were stepping out in faith, clinging to the hope that God would remove Chris's malady. Jan and I rested on God's divine power to move mountains and banked on a life-changing miracle. This unshakable faith of knowing God could and would work miracles in Chris's life supercharged our confidence. We were sure God was about to do something big—really big! When my daughter Diane asked me if Chris was going to die, I answered with a firm no, because both Jan and I strongly felt that God was going to do something absolutely spectacular in Chris's suffering. We sought the hand of the Lord, our Savior and friend, knowing He would be there and come through.

Confusion Personified

Our lives were being rocked at every turn. Chris's declining medical condition was a giant mystery. Her breathing problems intensified. Her blood counts continued to produce strange results the doctors could not identify. Chris's blood work was being sent to various hospitals in the Chicago area, as well as other hospitals around the country, in search of answers and input. The oncology staff at Children's was getting desperate. Chris's lead doctor was now Dr. Ruby. Dr. Lee had accepted another position at a children's hospital back east.

What a Fighter

It is very difficult for me to put into words just how complicated and unusual Chris's symptoms had become. Chris was aware of her deteriorating condition. She depended on oxygen more frequently. Her lack of appetite alarmed all of us. Chris grew weaker and weaker every day and then, it seemed, by the hour. She handled it all with an incredible strength and composure that could come only from God's unlimited resources. She was usually quite calm and never complained or panicked, even in the eye of this terrible storm that was swirling all around her. Chris was just a kid chronologically in terms of her ten and a half years on this earth. However, she was truly beyond her years emotionally, mentally, and spiritually. My intent here is not to make this a brag opportunity on behalf of my dying child. This was also the observation of some of her doctors and nurses who worked most closely with her. In many ways Chris kept us balanced as we witnessed her courage in the heat of the battle for her life.

The Lion and the Lamb

Scripture offers several titles for Jesus; among them are the Lion and the Lamb. For example, "You are a lion's cub, O Judah; you return from the prey, my Son. Like a lion He crouches and lies down, like a lioness—who dares to rouse Him?" (Genesis 49:9). Judah, one of the twelve tribes of Israel, is identified as a Lion. Out of the tribe of Judah the Messiah would come. In Revelation 5:5, the last book in the Bible, Jesus is called the Lion of Judah. When Jesus returns to earth at His second coming, He will not come back as a meek king but as the mighty, conquering King of Kings and Lord of Lords. The title "Lion" symbolizes His power and authority to destroy the forces of death, sin, and evil and usher in the New Jerusalem (2 Thessalonians 1:7–10). What a glorious time that will be for all believers in Christ.

In Revelation 5:6a Jesus is pictured as a lamb. "Then I saw a Lamb, looking as if it had been slain, standing in the center of the throne, encircled by the four living creatures and the elders." In OT prophecy the Lion Jesus was pictured as being the powerful, ultimate authority over all creation. He will conquer and reign forever and ever. Hallelujah! Amen! As the Lamb of God, Jesus was under the authority of God's perfect will and paid the ultimate price for humanity's sin and redemption. His sacrifice means He purchased every believer's one-way ticket to a wonderful place called heaven.

Telling It Like It Is

The prophet Isaiah prophesied about the Lamb of God hundreds of years before Jesus was born. He said, "He was oppressed and afflicted, yet He did not open His mouth; He was led like a lamb to the slaughter, and as a sheep before her shearers is silent, so He did not open His mouth" (Isaiah 53:7). Animal sacrifices for sin were commonplace in the OT. As the sinless Lamb of God, Jesus gave Himself for our sins. Jesus was falsely accused, mocked, abandoned, and beaten to a bloody pulp. Through all the humiliation and torture He did not complain once. When they nailed Him on a cross to die, He cried out, "Father, forgive them for they do not know what they are doing" (Luke 23:34). Jesus did all this for our sins and for the world's salvation. This truth was and still is His divine destiny.

Tunnel Vision

It is important that I share this background with the reader of this book, because God's message of salvation and eternal life became our focus and lifeline. We did not want to look to the right or to the left. With all our being, we tried to look upon our Lord and no one else. I ran across a bookmark that best explains where our faith was in that hospital some years ago and puts Chris's last days in spiritual perspective. It reads like this:

Lord like a filter over a camera lens

Let everything in my life
Be tinted by my focus on Christ.

Oh Lord, Give Us Strength for One More Day

Yes, there were times when we lamented and there were times when we just collapsed into tears. This sentence pretty much summed up our feelings and emotions. We kept reminding Chris and ourselves that no matter what happened, we had to fix our eyes on Jesus. It was in maintaining our focus on the Lord that we were able to face the inevitable in a few days. In our moments of weakness and doubt, we found the strength for each day by praising and worshipping God for His goodness and mercy, for what He had done for us in the past, what He was doing for us that day, and what He would do for us the next day and the next. We kept reaching out, trusting that Jesus was still in control regardless of what came our way.

Moving On

Each passing hour of the day was like experiencing a mighty wind of the Spirit in our midst. God had long moved us past basic Christianity 101. We were now promoted to a higher level, into an advanced spiritual realm, if you will. I'm not trying to come across as arrogant or boastful, but what we were experiencing was not for spiritual wimps. As I have said several times, God was preparing us for what was to come.

Confronting the Truth

Jan's prayer group knew all about the prophecy or God's "love letter" she had received about Chris's new birth. Their understanding of Chris's new birth was contrary to what Jan wanted for Chris. They knew it meant that Chris was going to die and go to heaven. She was not prepared to hear what they had to say and refused to accept their interpretation. Jan wanted to hold on to the hope that Chris would receive another miracle cure. Both Jan and I held on to the belief that Chris would receive this new birth, meaning a physical healing. By faith we claimed this healing right to the end.

Lord, It Hurts So Bad!

Our burning desire was for Chris to live a full life and be cured from this horrible disease. At the same time, we did not want to see our little girl suffer. We ached for her physical new birth. The time came when we prayed with our spiritual eyes and hearts wide open. For the first time we realized that Chris's new birth would be her reward of eternal life with Jesus. Regardless of what she had to endure, God had sealed her destiny. She would be with Him. It was a bittersweet revelation for us. We finally understood and accepted what our inner circle of Christian friends knew all along.

These Precious Moments

Approaching Chris's last days, Jan and I wanted to cherish every moment we had with Chris. As we moved in to her last week, my heart was hurting so badly, I just wanted to hold her and protect her. I wanted to pick her up and say, "Chrissy, everything is going to be okay. Mommy and Daddy are right here with you." Jan was still limited because of the blood clot. Knowing the baby was due at any time created some additional anxiety.

Now our focus and energies were on Chris. Being with her constantly was important to the three of us: Chris, Mom, and Dad. But our time was running out. The clock kept ticking, and we couldn't stop it. *Lord, please make the time go slower; make the hour hand stop! Let me kiss her a thousand times today! Let me tell her just how much I love her! Give me more time to let her know what a special gift she is to Mom, Dad,*

Connie, and Diane! God was gracious and allowed Jan and me to have those precious intimate moments.

Circus Peanuts

In the last three or four days, Chris could hardly eat solid food. We encouraged her to eat whatever she wanted. Chris loved those circus peanut candies. One evening, her supper tray was brought to her bed. She just couldn't eat. Instead she started munching on her circus peanuts. While Chris was trying to catch her breath between bites, a nurse came into the room and started complaining that Chris should be eating a balanced meal instead of eating candy. I must admit I was upset with the nurse's attitude about Chris's eating habits at this particular time. When the nurse left the room, Jan and I experienced a little of the old Chris. Her wrath boiled over. In her feisty manner, Chris defended her diet of circus peanuts. Laboring to speak, she finally responded, "Well, there is nothing wrong with eating circus peanuts. They also have nutritional value."

The time for Chris to be with her Lord was fast approaching.

Your trouble today can bring God's victory tomorrow.

"Just When I Needed You Most,"
Words by: Randy Vanwarmer and Tony Wilson
(Some lyrics paraphrased)

As you were packing your things, I was gazing out the
    window
I just couldn't find the right words to say.
You walked out the door into a storm
I did not try to stop you.

But I miss you now more than I could ever imagined.
God only knows where my strength and comfort will come
    from.
You walked out on me at a time when I really needed you.

So every morning I gaze out my window
And wonder where you are.
I have put some words in a letter that I would like to mail to
    you.
I hope you will mail a letter to me.

For my need for you has never been greater.
I don't know where my strength and comfort will come
    from.
You walked out on me at a time when I really needed you.

CHAPTER ELEVEN

"Just When I Needed You Most"

Our Plans and Dreams Were Fading

It was now the last week of Chris's life, but we didn't realize it. We were running out of time and memories to share with her. These paraphrased words from "Just When I Needed You Most" bring back memories of just how desperate we were. I miss you now more than I ever could have imagined. God only knows where my strength will come from. Jan's medical condition with the blood clot was becoming critical. Her doctor along with friends urged her to stay home and off her leg. For the next three days, I was with Chris at the hospital. As I reflect on those precious few days, they had by far the greatest effect on my life. I was faced with the staggering reality that Chris was not going to be miraculously healed. I basically asked Jesus for the strength, wisdom, and courage to minister to my little baby girl in the time we had left.

The Details Under Control

God had blessed us in so many ways leading up to these crises moments. Our friends and church family took care of many details for us, which enabled us to spend as much time with Chris as possible. The middle management at Jewel was very supportive and understanding of my situation. At the time, I was market manager for a Jewel Food

Store in Saint Charles. A small-volume market and crew enabled me to be absent from work without major problems. Paul said, "Rejoice in the Lord always, I will say it again: Rejoice! Let your gentleness be evident to all. The Lord is near. Do not be anxious about anything, but in everything, by prayer and petition, with thanksgiving, present your requests to God. And the peace of God, which transcends all understanding, will guard your hearts and your minds in Christ Jesus" (Philippians 4:4–7).

Paul was reminding believers that if Jesus Christ is with you every day, it becomes easier to obey him. When we are rejoicing in the Lord, our lives are centered on Him. Rejoicing in the Lord means recognizing that He is always near, always one prayer, one question, and one cry away. Therefore, we find peace with God by standing firm in Christ regardless of what is going on in our lives. It is when we can come to Jesus with sincere worship and let Him search our inner thoughts that we discover this wonderful life-changing truth; He will meet all our needs! The antidote for worry and fear is enjoying the loving presence of Christ. Hebrews 13:8 reminds us that Jesus is unchanging. *What Jesus can do for you now, He will also do for you later.*

Always There

Throughout our ordeal, we sought the Lord. Did we make mistakes get frustrated, angry and fearful along the way? Absolutely! Yet God always was gracious, forgiving, and patient with us. We often rejoiced even in the midst of the trials, because we knew Jesus would not forsake us. We weren't overly anxious about the logistics surrounding Chris's care, for we knew God was in control. Now, this might sound a bit naïve or like an exaggeration, or it might be hard for some to believe, but it was true in our case. I just cannot say it enough. We constantly sought the presence of the Lord in our decisions and petitions.

Please! Please! Give Us Some Answers

Chris's concentration would drift now and then, almost as though she wasn't paying attention. Then suddenly she would have an increased awareness of what was going on around her. This had been taking place since she had had her seizure in late January. Chris found it very difficult to fall into a deep sleep for long periods of time. She was restless because of a lack of oxygen. The doctors could not maintain Chris's oxygen at normal breathing levels. Her frail body was slowly shutting down. Yet we still did not have answers to why all this madness was happening. Hour after hour I waited, hoping the doctors would give us a clue, some kind of answer that would turn her deteriorating condition around. The agony of wondering continued. We had so many questions and so few answers. *What is going on, God?* we asked. *Please, Lord, we need some answers and we need them fast!*

The Evil One

There is not one person walking on the face of this earth who is exempt from various trials and afflictions. The devil is not some mythical figure holding a pitchfork in his hand and with two horns sticking out of his ugly head. The fact is that Satan is not a symbol, fairy-tale figure, or legend. Friends, he is as real as the nose on your face. The Devil is a fallen angel, the public enemy of God and of all that is good. Through his own pride, he became corrupt. God defeated him and cast him out of heaven. The Devil is a murderer, deceiver, accuser, and our main adversary. As human beings we do not possess the means to counter or defeat him. His main goal is to rob us of our eternal destination, heaven. The bottom line is that he wants you and me to burn in hell with him. Both day and night he is at work trying to hinder God's work.

Overmatched

The apostle Paul reminds us how we can overcome. "Finally, be strong in the Lord and in His mighty power. Put on the armor of God so that you can take your stand against the devil's schemes. For our struggle is not against flesh and blood, but against the rulers, against the authorities, against the powers of this dark world and against the spiritual forces of evil in Heavenly realms" (Ephesians 6:10-12).

Paul gives us a very sobering reminder of our number one enemy. He is strong, and far more powerful than the flesh. We overcome Satan by the power of Jesus' blood shed on the cross. Paul encourages us to remain strong. Where do we find the strength to resist temptation, and to fight and resist Satan's attacks? We do so by standing firm in Christ, reading and applying His Word. We need to embrace this truth. Almighty God is available to every believer through the indwelling power of the Holy Spirit. There is no other way to stand against powerful evil forces, period. Satan is out to seek and destroy every person who walks on this earth. Paul said he is the ruler of darkness and uses deception and lies to overpower us.

Hanging On to Jesus

John, under the inspiration of the Holy Spirit, said, "Then I heard a loud voice in Heaven say: Now have come the salvation and the power of the Kingdom of our God, and the authority of His Christ. For the accuser of our brothers, who accuses them before our God day and night, has been hurled down. They overcame him by the blood of the Lamb (Christ) and the Word (Bible) of their testimony; they did not love their lives so much as to shrink from death" (Revelation 12:10-11). These verses tell us Satan has been kicked out of heaven. His ultimate demise would come at the hands of the Lamb Jesus, who shed His blood for humanity's sins and death.

Wednesday

I was frantically hanging on to Jesus more than ever Wednesday evening. Chris had been in a ward with other children. Her condition was downgraded to critical. Jan was still confined at home because of her blood clot. I was faced with the hardest trial of my married life. I am not in the least ashamed to say that I was flat out scared and worried. In the midst of my fears, I reached out once again to Jesus. I understood that the ultimate victory was found in Him. This powerful truth gave me courage and hope for what I would face through the night. I hung on to His promises recorded in the Word, believing we would be victorious over every trial and affliction that came our way, even while I was shaking in my boots.

Daddy's Time

Chris became increasingly uncomfortable, laboring for more air. Finally, she was able to settle down a bit. I pulled up a chair next to her bed, with my Bible opened on my lap. I told her Mommy would come and see her tomorrow, Thursday. Chris looked forward to her mom's visit. It had been a few days since she had seen Jan. But for now, it was Chris and Dad. What took place during Chris's last night on this earth was something I will always remember and cherish in my heart. It was truly a God-anointing time for both of us.

Again some of the words paraphrased from the song by Rick Roberts, "Just Remember I Love You," draw me back to that night alone with my precious daughter.

> When pain and trouble comes your way
> And you just want to lie down and cry.
> When the world around you is falling apart
> And you cannot understand why it's happening.

And you don't understand where your strength and
   comfort will come from
All your hopes and dreams have vanished and friends have
   disappointed you.
I want you to remember I love you more than words can
   express.

That Loving Feeling

After eleven o'clock the other children in Chris's ward had settled down for the night. As I sat next to Chris, she wanted me to
scratch her arms and legs. Throughout the night I kept scratching
my dying daughter's arms and legs. She would wake up, we would
talk briefly, she would ask if I would continue scratching her, and
then she would fall back to sleep. At times during the night I would
pray and read the Word to her. As she slept, I kept reading from
God's Word, seeking His peace and comfort. Chris began losing
control of her bodily functions. Even in the midst of her extreme
discomfort, she was concerned about me being inconvenienced
when she had an accident. In those moments I loved her more than
words could possibly express. Her faith during this time was simple
but profound. I truly believe God gave Chris an extra dose of faith
in her remaining hours. I had never felt so close to Chris as I did
on that precious night, when God was gracious and allowed us to
squeeze in a lifetime of memories. I loved you more than I can ever
say, Chrissy.

Mommy's Here

That same Wednesday, Jan boldly went to her doctor and told
him she was going down to Children's Memorial Hospital to be
with Chris and there would be no room for discussion. She had
not seen Chris for three days because of the condition surrounding

her pregnancy. Her doctor relented. He figured if she had the baby while being with Chris, at least she would be in a hospital. It brought Chris great comfort knowing that Mommy was coming to be with her.

Reality Sets In

The next day, our pastor, the Reverend Tom Estes, drove Jan to Children's Memorial Hospital in Chicago. They arrived at approximately ten o'clock Thursday morning. Jan was startled to find that the staff was in the process of moving Chris into a private room closer to the nurses' station. Both of us knew what that meant. We called it the "death room." Jan was not prepared for this moment. Part of her heart was still clinging to Chris's new birth, not death. After spending that previous night with Chris, I realized that she was not going to survive and would die soon. When Chris was settled in her single room, Dr. Hruby, Chris's primary oncology doctor, along with other staff members took us to the conference room to tell us Chris was dying. They could not give us a definitive reason why since all the recent blood tests showed that she was still in remission. So what was going on?

Family's Last Good-bye

Pastor Tom stayed with us for a while. Jan and I made a series of phone calls to family and friends, updating them on Chris's grave condition. Jan's parents, along with her brother and sister-in-law, arrived at the hospital around midday to say their good-byes. It was very painful to watch Jan's parents share their last words with Chris. They were so overwhelmed with grief.

A Brief Moment of Laughter

At one point during the day, Jan read to Chris her favorite Scripture verses from Psalm 27. As Jan began reading verse 4, "One thing I ask of the Lord: this is what I seek," Chris interrupted and said, "Air," and then laughed. Chris was struggling for every breath. What we didn't know at the time was that her lungs were filled with cancer.

Just the Four of Us

It was approaching ten o'clock Thursday evening. The remaining members of our family had left the hospital. Now it was just the four of us: Jesus, Jan, Chris, and myself. The staff had set up two cots in Chris's room, one on each side of her bed. Chris's breathing was becoming increasingly irregular, and her sleep was sporadic. She would wake in a fretful state, asking for more morphine to help her rest. Finally the doctors agreed, but they cautioned us that it could hasten her death. At our request, they gave Chris more morphine in her IV. A short time later, Chris spoke her last words: "Oh, Mommy, it's working. Thank You, Jesus, praise You, Jesus, thank You, Jesus." Then she went to sleep. This all took place around ten thirty that night.

Words of Wisdom

It was approaching midnight. The trauma of the day kept Jan on her feet more than the medical staff advised. Finally, Jan lay down on her cot on the left side of Chris's bed. In the meantime, I was leaning against the wall just outside Chris's room. Walking down the hall toward me was a rather tall young man. He stopped, looked at me, and said, "I think you could use a cup of coffee." We went down to the coffee shop. This young man was a seminary student who had just finished his shift as chaplain intern for Children's

Memorial Hospital. We spoke for a brief period of time. I did most of the talking while he listened carefully. Then I said, "I don't want my daughter to die, but I don't want her to suffer either." The young intern's response soon changed my life forever. He set aside all the theological jargon and pat answers and simply said to me, "You don't know what is around the corner of your daughter's life, but God does. He knows what is best for your daughter. Maybe you should just pray that God's will be done in her life."

Perfect Timing

By then it was approaching twelve thirty on Friday morning. I thanked the chaplain for taking the time to listen. I went back to Chris's room. I encouraged Jan to rest on her cot. Chris was resting, but her breathing was becoming very shallow. I lay down on my cot on the right side of Chris's bed. As I lay on my back, I remembered what the young chaplain had said to me a few minutes earlier.

With tears streaming down both sides of my face, I began praying, "Lord, I love Chris. I don't want her to die, but You know what is best for her, so Lord, I pray that your will be done in Chris's life." The very instant (not seconds) I finished that prayer, Chris stopped breathing. God's timing was perfect. In a split second, Jan rose from her cot and hurried past Chris's bed, moving as swiftly as she could toward the door, saying, "Chris stopped breathing!"

As Jan rushed past me, I reached out and gently took her by the arm and said, "I know, Jan. It's all right."

She looked into my eyes and responded, "Yes, it is." Then she quietly and slowly approached the nurses' station and informed them that Chris had died. Christine Carol Carr, at the age of ten years and six months, went to be with her precious Lord at approximately twelve thirty a.m. on March 25, 1977.

Death Is Swallowed Up in Victory

I never felt the presence of the Lord more than I did when Chris took her last breath. God was absolutely right on time! Only God could have intervened at such a dramatic moment. The week before Chris died, our church's Sunday bulletin, when unfolded, had a picture of a beautiful butterfly saying, "Behold I make all things new" (Revelation 21:5). Chris liked it so much; she wanted it taped to her television set in her hospital room. Both Jan and I knew without a shred of doubt that Chris had finally experienced her new birth with Jesus. I must be honest. The convicting, comforting Holy Spirit was all over Chris's room at the time of her death. The ugly stench of death was swallowed up in victory. Jesus, the Lamb of God, was once again victorious!

Divine Proclamation

We read these awesome, uplifting, life-changing words, "Death has been swallowed up in victory. Where, O death, is your victory? Where, O death is your sting? The sting of death is sin, and the power of sin is the law. But thanks be to God! He gives us the victory through our Lord Jesus Christ" (1 Corinthinas 15:54–56). It might appear to some that death means Satan has won. Nothing could be further from the truth! Satan is doomed for destruction; his power and influence will not last. He began his evil work against humanity during creation and continues his pursuit to inflict pain, corruption, and even death on our bodies and souls today. But his day is coming. God will eternally seal his fate and throw him into the lake of fire where he belongs. Then God will be victorious over evil once and for all!

Death, Where Is Your Sting?

Pastor Randal Ross, senior pastor of Calvary Church in Naperville, Illinois, in his inspiring book *From the Cross to Eternity* shares the story of when Tony Campolo went to the funeral of his sixteen-year-old friend Clarence. He listened to the pastor preach on John 14:1: "Do not let our hearts be troubled. Trust in God; trust also in Me." Campolo said, "I knew the joy of the Lord, a joy that, in the face of death, laughs and sings, for there is no sting in death."

Pastor Ross' comments on Tony Campolo's story spoke directly to what Jan and I felt as we stood over Chris's body that night.

> The clock of our sorrow is coming to an end, and a good day is ahead. The clock is ticking and what is coming will be worth waiting for. We are like the child waiting for Christmas or a birthday party. The clock seems to move so slowly. But the moment will come when joy breaks-forth with a time to celebrate and receive eternal life. All of us who have received Him will share in His proclamation of victory: It is finished!

Praise God, there will be no sting of death for those who have received Jesus as Lord and Savior. Chris was victorious! Jesus had removed her sting of death, praise Jesus. We experienced this joyful truth in her hospital room on March 25.

How About You?

Let me ask this question. Please be honest with yourself as you answer. Are you absolutely sure, confident, that you will one day be united with Jesus in eternity? It is so crucial for us to understand this following truth. God has written the final chapter of your life and my life. God has been around every corner of every life. Eternity with

Jesus brings satisfaction, purpose, and fulfillment for all those who have personally received Jesus as Lord and Savior in their hearts.

Just Give Me the Facts

Some might say they need more details before they will believe, but we have enough information in the Bible to know that eternity with God in Christ will be in a real place that is rewarding, magnificent, and exciting beyond our wildest dreams. The exact moment I prayed, "Lord I want Your will to be done," my daughter was united with her mighty Lord. Her wonderful eternity had just begun. Chris went to a real place where God wiped away the tears from her eyes. She will never experience another IV, bone marrow test, spinal tap, or blood transfusion. Her pain and sorrow have disappeared forever and ever. Amen!

You're Not Alone

Permit me to just say this before I get back to Chris's room on the night she died. If you are a Christian, whatever it is you are going through, and no matter how traumatic or how devastating your trials and afflictions are, they will not have the last word. For Jesus said, "Never will I leave you; never will I forsake you" (Hebrews 13:5). Yes, God has a very special place prepared for you, a place that defies any human description. God in Christ will dwell with you there personally. His glorious light of majesty will replace your darkness or night. Darkness or night in the Bible symbolizes death, sin, pain, sorrow, and fear. These things will be nonexistent in God's heavenly city, our eternal dwelling place. "The Lord will rescue me from every evil attack and will bring me safely to His Heavenly Kingdom. To Him be glory for ever and ever AMEN" (2 Timothy 4:18). *Trusting in Jesus' authority should be the believer's priority.*

The Afterglow

When Jan came back into Chris's room after informing the nursing staff, I was standing over Chris's bed. Jan joined me. A short time later, two doctors and a nurse entered. I calmly asked the doctors if they would remove all the needles and the IV from Chris's body, and turn off the oxygen. As the doctors were removing the needles, I looked down on Chris's lifeless body and she just glowed. Jan and I began singing praise songs to the Lord as we looked down upon our Chrissy. This was unusual since I have never been one to sing out loud with others listening. The doctors looked at us as if we had just gone over the edge. But the truth was that we were just so much in the presence of the Lord. As I gazed at my daughter, I realized I had never felt so proud and blessed to have the privilege of being her daddy. I was thankful that God had given us the gift of Chris for more than ten years and for His grace of providing what we needed at the time of her death.

Returning Home

We picked up Connie and Diane at four in the morning at the Seidels' house. We put the girls in our king-sized bed and told them their sister was now with the Lord. The girls cried, and we comforted them as best we could. We just held on to each other. I was never so proud and thankful for our two little girls as I was on that early morning, March 25. Connie and Diane had gone through so much at such a young age. I was also never so proud of and thankful for my very pregnant and overdue wife. I was never so proud of a mom who had remained incredibly strong in the Lord in the midst of a horrible, devastating struggle. I was never so proud of a mom who had cared for her dying daughter to the very end. God placed a deepened love in my heart for my family, at the time of Chris's death. The rest of the morning we all slept together, with Jan and I cuddling our two daughters, all the while seeking Jesus' comfort and strength in the midst of our tears.

Holy, Holy, Holy

"The Revelation Song," written by Jennie Len Riddle, reminds me that we are never alone night and day in our grief, pain, and sorrow. May some of these paraphrased words from this wonderful and inspiring song speak to your heart in your dark hour of need. May they give you a renewed hope and promise of a new and better day. Remember, you are never alone no matter what affliction you are going through.

> "The Revelation Song"
> Words by: Jennie Lee Riddle
> (Some lyrics paraphrased)
>
> Holy, Holy, Holy
> Is the Lord God Almighty
> Who was, and is, and is to come!
> Along with the world, I deliver a song
> Glorify to the Lord of Lords!
> Lord, You are my all
> And I worship You
>
> Dressed in multi colors caused by rays of
> Raindrops
> All praise, adoration, power, and wonder
> Fill Your being, oh worthy master

God not only sees us for who we are now, but who we can be.

"Having My Baby"
Words by: by Paul Anka
(Some lyrics paraphrased)

Having our child is a tender way of expressing
Your devotion to me and how much I am on your mind.

Your radiance is so clear to me.
Your eyes are sparkling.
It makes me rejoice that you also see it.
You're giving birth to my child.
I love you and how this experience is affecting you.

Having our child reveals your love for me.
What is happening to you warms my heart.

The life that is welling up in you is revealing.
Darling, do you sense this child coming alive?
Are you full of joy that you are having my child?

I am happy to have your baby because I love you.
Your love is evident by the child that is growing inside of
    you.
I can't think of a better way of expressing our devotion
Than by having my child.

CHAPTER TWELVE

"Having My Baby"

Still Searching for Answers

Since Chris had been a participant in the research program at Children's Memorial Hospital, Dr. Hruby requested our approval for an autopsy. We affirmed her request in hopes of finding not only the cause of her death, but any additional medical information from her case that might be beneficial to other children fighting leukemia and other cancers.

Making Plans

That Friday afternoon after Chris's death, we made the funeral arrangements. Jan's OB-GYN and the funeral home staff advised that we have the visitation the next day—Saturday afternoon—and the funeral Sunday, earlier than normal because of Jan's pregnancy. The doctor had real concerns about Jan and the baby's health, coupled with the emotional loss of Chris and the upcoming memorial service. The fact that Jan was overdue just added more stress to an already traumatic situation. We were making preparations for our daughter's funeral and at the same time planning for our new arrival. We were also facing life-risking issues for Jan and the baby. To say we were numb because of our unusual circumstances was an understatement.

Seeking Guidance

Once again we reached out to Jesus for guidance. The plain truth is that if we hadn't, there was no way we would have been able to get through the coming days with our sanity intact. Paul said,

> For this reason, since the day we heard about you, we have not stopped praying for you asking God to fill you with the knowledge of His will through all Spiritual wisdom and understanding. And we pray this in order that you may live a life worthy of the Lord and may please Him in every way: bearing fruit in every good work, growing in the knowledge of God, being strengthened with all the power according to His glorious might so that you may have great endurance and patience, and joyfully giving thanks to the Father, who has qualified you to share in the inheritance of the saints in the Kingdom of light. (Colossians 1:9–12)

Walking with Him

Paul's prayer was centered on the hope that the Colossians would be filled with God's power, wisdom, knowledge, and understanding. As they grew in the knowledge of God, they would bear good, productive fruit. The knowledge of God produces patience and endurance. We desperately needed Jesus to help us endure, especially in the coming days. We sought Spiritual wisdom to experience His glorious power in every coming decision we had to face. *Jesus our daily bread feeds our spiritual needs.*

Just in Time

My brother Steve and his wife, Sharon, came to our home early Friday evening at just the right time. What a blessing it was for Jan,

Connie, Diane, and me to have them with us at such a difficult and vulnerable period of our lives. Their coming was truly an answer to prayer. They took some of our burdens and placed them upon themselves, for which we are forever grateful.

It's Getting Close

The morning after Chris's death, Saturday, March 26, our sister in-law Sharon took Jan, Connie, and Diane shopping for tights for our little girls. Jan began having labor pains and decided to stay in the car while Sharon took the girls into the store. Jan prayed, asking the Lord to give her thirty-six more hours so she could go to Chris's memorial service on Sunday, March 27. Jan's labor continued on and off the rest of the day.

The Visitation

Chris's visitation was held at three o'clock on Saturday, March 26. This was the first time Connie and Diane had seen Chris in two weeks. We took the girls by their little hands and escorted them to the casket. They asked to touch Chris's body. Six-year-old Diane touched Chris and said, "That's not her. Where did she go?" Jan and I were very intentional and sensitive regarding the girls' psychological and spiritual well-being at such young ages. Our plan was to minister to them by explaining Chris's death in ways they could understand. We did not want them growing up fearing death. I said, "This is Chris's earthly body, but she will have a new body in heaven. Chrissy is now with Jesus."

Conversation on the Cross

We recall Jesus' conversation with two criminals on the cross. One insulted Jesus. "But the other criminal rebuked him. Don't you fear God, he said, since you are under the same sentence? We are pun-ished justly, for we are getting what our deeds deserve. But this man had done nothing wrong. Then he said, Jesus, remember me when you come into your kingdom. Jesus answered him, I tell you the truth, today you will be with Me in paradise" (Luke 23:40-43).

The Lord had compassion for one thief who believed, and ush-ered him into salvation at just the right moment. This dying thief looked beyond his present pain, looming death and asked Jesus to remember Him when He entered His kingdom. We tried to keep the theology of death plain and simple for the girls, in hopes that what we shared would help them process Chris's death in their own way. We wanted them to understand that like the proclamation of a dying thief, Chris was now with Jesus in paradise, and that her pain and suffering was over.

Break Out the Candy and Cigars

After Chris's visitation was over, we decided to go out for supper. Jan called her doctor. He agreed to meet her at the hospital around seven o'clock that evening. In the meantime, Jan's parents took us to a nice restaurant for supper. It was uncomfortable for Jan to sit because the baby was so low. After our unusual dinner, Jan's parents took Connie and Diane home while I drove Jan to the hospital. The doctor's initial plan was to induce her labor, but he did not have to. I began praying to the Lord that Jan and the baby would be healthy. I also prayed that if we had another girl, she would be healthy. Then I added, "But Lord, I really want a son." Another prophecy of Jan's love letter was about to be fulfilled. Our son, David Joseph Carr, was born Saturday night at 9:17 on March 26, less then forty-eight hours after Chris had died. The celebration had begun, although we had mixed emotions. We were overjoyed with the birth of our son while grieving over the loss of our daughter Chris.

Finding Mercy and Grace

We knew our only hope was to be found in the goodness and grace of God. Lamentations 3:25 reads, "The Lord is good to those whose hope is in Him, to the one who seeks Him."

Jeremiah was in the middle of a great storm filled with pain, sorrow, and hardship, for himself and his people. However, his life and perspective turned around when he sought the Lord in his time of stress. He knew that no matter what, God would not fail him. He put his trust in God's faithfulness. Thus, Jeremiah discovered God's mercy, and God responded to his cry. By His mercy and unlimited grace, God embraced and spared the remnant of Judah. He was there for the Israelites and blessed them through years of captivity. Eventually God allowed them to return and rebuild their city and temple.

Calling Out to God

We weren't trying to be "superheroes" in the faith. The truth was that we were emotionally drained. Yes, without a doubt God showed up in a supernatural way when Chris died. We leaned on the Lord, trusting in His miraculous intervention. This truth did not change the fact that our human side was torn apart by losing Chris. Fear for Jan's health and the baby's was a real concern because of the stressful circumstances that surrounded David's birth. We certainly lacked the personal resources to make things better, but we knew of a mighty God who could. Like Jeremiah, in our time of turmoil, we called out to God and waited upon His favor. We simply asked and put our trust in God's faithfulness in the midst of a raging storm that was beating at the very doors of our hearts and minds. In particular we called on God's mercy and promises in Christ to see us through.

Beat the Clock

After David's birth, Jan hemorrhaged, but her goal was to attend Chris's memorial service the following day, at two o'clock in the afternoon of Sunday, March 27. Now, getting the doctor's permission to attend her daughter's service was a challenge. The doctor made a deal with Jan. If she could stand up on her own by midnight, she could go to her daughter's service. The first couple of times Jan tried to stand up by herself, she fainted. By the grace of God she was able to stand on her feet ten minutes before twelve! How we praised the Lord for all things, even Jan being able to stand up without assistance.

The Gathering

Jan arrived at Chris's memorial service from the hospital in a wheelchair. The sanctuary at Fox Valley Presbyterian Church in Geneva had standing room only. People were standing in stairways leading down to the fellowship hall. People filled the narthex and spilled out into the parking lot. I mention this not to brag or boast, but only to offer our deepest love and respect for those who took the time to minister to us by their presence in our greatest hour of grief. We were truly humbled by the response from so many wonderful and caring people.

Surprise

Some people were surprised by Jan's reaction at Chris's memorial service. They thought she was in "shock" because she could rejoice in David's birth even though Chris had died. It was difficult for some to comprehend Jan's response that day. It was the wonderful, amazing, sweet, gentle Holy Spirit that finally convinced Jan of Chris's new birth. Jan knew without a shred of doubt that Chris was with Jesus.

This awesome truth sustained and gave us hope and strength beyond human measure in the coming months.

The End of a Long Day

The memorial service and reception was behind us. I had to take Jan back to the hospital. We reflected on the events of the day. It was extremely difficult, making the transition from one emotion to another. The joy of having a new addition to the family was awesome. However, the pain of Chris's loss stung. One moment we were joyful and the next was pure heartbreak. These roller-coaster feelings would be with us for some time. The next day, Monday, March 28, Jan had to have surgery to prevent her from having more children. If she became pregnant again, another blood clot could jeopardize her life and the baby's as well.

The Fabulous Three

During those days, God placed three very special Christian friends in Jan's life: Beth Luther, Carol Seidel, and Sandy Petrille. God used these three women in mighty ways. They were not only united in the Lord together, but invested much of themselves in Jan's journey with Chris. With Jan in the hospital a few extra days after David's birth, they came to visit and cheer her up. Jan said, "They had me laughing so hard, I had to send them home." When they left, Jan's roommate commented on what wonderful friends she had and how full of love they were. They laughed together, shared together, and cried together. Proverbs 17:22 reminds us, "A cheerful heart is good medicine." Beth, Carol, and Sandy provided just the right dose of laughter that Jan needed at the time. What a privilege and blessing to have such wonderful, faithful friends!

Hidden Pain

Connie and Diane were in very good hands during those times when we were away from them because of Chris's illness. However, Diane shared with me years later how painful it was for her and Connie. She said they felt loved and taken care of, but missed Mom and Dad. Diane also shared that after Chris died, she was in constant fear. One night Connie and Diane came to see their new little brother in the hospital. When Diane did not see her mom, she thought, Did Mom die too? For months she feared that something bad was going to happen and David was going to die. The girls possessed a great ability for their ages to hide such fear from us. They also did not want to add to Mom and Dad's burdens or "make us feel sad."

Those Dark and Lonely Nights

The next few weeks were filled with mixed blessings for sure. The grieving process was difficult, as most of us know when we experience the loss of a loved one. The pain becomes especially acute when we are alone at night with our thoughts and memories. We were surrounded by many wonderful Christians who helped us deal with the hard times. I also had my work. During the day Jan and I were both preoccupied with trying to get our lives back to some kind of normal. There were times when Jan would be nursing David and then suddenly be overwhelmed with tears, thinking of Chris.

The first few weeks were especially difficult for me. I dreaded crawling into bed at night, because I knew what was to come. With no distractions, I would be alone with my hidden thoughts. That is when my grief surrounding Chris's loss would hit me the hardest and most deeply. I would lie there in the darkness overcome with sadness and yearning to see Chris again. At that moment I would pray, "Lord, I'm hurting and devastated. I miss Chrissy so much. Please take this pain from me, Lord." When I finished that prayer, the Holy Spirit would give me instant relief from my agony and loneliness. God would always replace my despair with Jesus' peace and comfort. Once again His timing was perfect. *Approaching God's throne is better than going it alone.*

Relief from Despair

Perhaps you are afflicted because of persecution, loss of a job, rejection, health, relationship problems, financial concerns, loneliness, depression, or loss of a loved one. Whatever your darkest hour might be, remember that there is a loving, caring Savior who understands your pain. Jesus desperately wants you to cry out to Him where you are. He wants you to lean on Him and not on someone else. It all comes down to this truth: only Jesus can bring you out of the depths of despair and darkness into a glorious, wonderful peace and hope.

"You Light Up My Life"

Someone (source unknown) once said about the song "You Light Up My Life," sung by Debby Boone and written by Joseph Brooks, "The song celebrates the essence of love which beams radiant at the darkest hours of life and gives the gifts of hope and happiness. Love is the deepest and most sought after feeling which gives you the strength to carry on in those times when the road you trudge seems to be uphill. It is the feeling that binds people into unity; it is not a fallacy but a reality that becomes the fabric of our lives."

The paraphrased words to "You Light Up My Life" for me speak of the light and love of Christ that illuminates hope, mercy, and grace in our darkest hour. Please read and reflect on their meaning. May they bring hope and purpose to your life.

"You Light Up My Life"
Words by: Joseph Brooks

(Some lyrics paraphrased)

Some evenings near my window I would
Hope for a song to be sung to me.
I have kept a host of dreams within myself until you came
     to me.

You have brightened my world
And have given me the will to continue on.
Your light has surrounded my days
And blessed my evenings with music.

Tossed by the waves, drifting aimlessly on the waters
Could this be leading me home?
I have been given the opportunity to express my love for
     you.
My lonely days have come to an end.

You have brightened my world.
You have given me the will to continue on.
You light has surrounded my days
And blessed my evenings with music.

What is happening to me cannot be a mistake
Because what I am feeling is real.
All I know is you have brightened my world.

One True Light

In my darkest hour of despair, the light and love of Christ gave me hope and comfort. Jesus said, "I am the light of the world. Whoever follows Me will never walk in darkness, but will have the light of life" (John 8:12). Jesus is our source of true light. Jesus' light causes darkness to disappear. Darkness in Scripture speaks of evil, sin, and death. Light symbolizes life, peace, protection, love, and joy—all that is good and profitable. Jesus wants us to follow His light, a light that will never be extinguished. He does not want us to walk in hopeless darkness. *Jesus will never abandon us in our hour of need.*

Moving On

God did not love us more than anyone else. We were a typical young, struggling family like so many others. We just learned how to submit to the Lordship of Jesus Christ who broke the chains of Chris's death. In a period of approximately three years, Jesus Christ literally became the very air we breathed. Our experiences with our dying daughter taught us one very important truth that we clung to every day. *Only Jesus can mend a wounded and broken heart.*

Looking Back

Reviewing Jan's journals about Chris's illness in preparation for writing this book truly confirms what I shared in the previous paragraph. It was very evident how we depended on the touch of Jesus one day at a time. We placed it all—our children, our hopes, our dreams, and our future—on the sovereignty of Almighty God.

Please Throw Us a Life Preserver

These verses from Isaiah best summarize how God came to our rescue time after time. He gave us the strength, courage, and hope to press on every day. It is my prayer that in your trials, this passage will also inspire and give you strength, courage, and hope to press on. "Even youths grow tired and weary, and young men stumble and fall; but those who hope in the Lord will renew their strength. They will soar on wings like eagles; they will run and not grow weary, they will walk and not be faint" (Isaiah 40:30-31).

Don't Look to Self

The prophet Isaiah gives us strong advice. Take your eyes off yourself and your problems, and fix them on God in Christ. For God can and will pour out all the strength you will ever need to sustain you in your time of weariness. We had come to realize how true the prophet's words were. In our weakness we became stronger in Christ. We simply placed our trust in the promise that He would be our supernatural source. When we thought we could not continue, God would renew our faith. He put us on His back and carried us so that we would not grow weary and not faint in discouragement. Praise You, Jesus, praise You, Lord, You are truly amazing and faithful! *Instead of surrendering to despair, we need to stand firm with confidence knowing God will deliver.*

Without Jesus we are left with nothing, but with Him we have everything.

"That's What Friends Are For"
Words by: Carol Bayer Sager and Burt Bacharach
(Some lyrics paraphrased)

In my wildest dreams I never thought I would have such
    feelings.
I am so grateful to have the chance to express my love for
    you.

If there would come a time when I had to go
Try to think about how we both feel right now
Then try and recall.

So continue to grin and glow
Believing without a doubt I will always be there for you.
That's what friendship is all about.

Those moments when we are separated
Just pause, reflect, and understand
What I am saying comes from the depths of my heart.

So continue to grin and glow
Believing without a doubt I will always be there for you.

Continue to grin and glow
Believing without a doubt I will always be there for you
Because that is what friendship is all about.

Through thick or thin
I will always be there for you.

CHAPTER THIRTEEN

"That's What Friends Are For"

What a Group!

From day one of Chris's diagnosis, we had the support of our family, friends, and church. I could dedicate pages to those who were there for us. Through thick and thin, our church family always came through on our behalf. They had our backs every step of the way. The outreach that was demonstrated by the people in our home church, Fox Valley Presbyterian Church in Geneva, epitomized the NT church recorded in the book of Acts. The church's endless ministry to the Carr family in our time of extreme need was simply incredible. We were so blessed, the song "That's What Friends Are For" really applied to this church. We shall never forget their acts of love and generosity. We will forever treasure our memories of them "in the heat of our battle."

The Message

The early Christian church was formed in the book of Acts. It would become the primary tool by which God would reveal His purpose to humankind. In Acts 10 the apostle Peter was at the home of Roman centurion Cornelius. While there, Peter preached a simple but powerful message. His brief words represented a clear and direct summarization of the gospel. Peter proclaimed that God anointed Jesus with the power of the Holy Spirit, and Jesus went around serving, healing, and doing good. He died on a cross and was resurrected. Peter shared that he and others were witnesses to Jesus' death and resurrection. The Lord Himself commanded Peter to preach and testify that Jesus was indeed the Christ who rose from the dead. God has appointed Jesus to judge the living as well as the dead. All who believe Jesus as Lord and Savior will receive forgiveness of their sins. Peter preached the necessity for all to embrace Jesus Christ as their personal Lord and Savior. *Jesus our daily bread feeds our spiritual needs.*

Nasty Strategy

Satan has a fivefold strategy for our lives based on the five Ds:

Delusion: He wants us to believe God is an illusion and add to our confusion.

Denial: He wants us to reject God's reign and focus on our pain.

Destroy: He wants to take away our fulfillment and replace it with his defilement.

Discouragement: He wants us to dwell on our frustration rather than on our salvation.

Deception: He wants to trick us into thinking God's promises will not stick.

Telling It Like It Is

The Bible I read says that if we believe Jesus Christ is Lord and Savior, if we believe Jesus is the incarnate resurrected Son of God, then there is only one church of Christ. It does not matter in the least if we attend and worship in a formal, informal, high, low, or anything-in-between church. If Jesus Christ *rocks* in your church and the God of

Abraham, Jacob, and Isaac is glorified, then the Holy Spirit is moving in the hearts, minds, and lives within your church.

No Place Like Home

My home church certainly embraced many qualities set forth in the book of Acts. They lived out Jesus' example of love and servanthood beyond what my words could ever possibly express. The writer of Ecclesiastes wrote,

> Again I saw something meaningless under the sun: There was a man all alone; he had neither son nor brother. There was no end to his toil, yet his eyes were not content with his wealth. For whom am I toiling, he asked, and why am I depriving myself of enjoyment? This too is meaningless—a miserable business! Two are better than one, because they have a good return for their work: If one falls down, his friend can help him up. But pity the man who falls and has no one to help him up. (Ecclesiastes 4:7–10)

Always There

I believe the writer of chapter 4 in Ecclesiastes was referring to something more than riches or accumulation of wealth. It's also about others coming alongside us in our time of need. It is not necessary for us to toil alone in this life. Sometimes we let our pride get in the way of asking for or accepting assistance from not only God, but also others. Unwillingness to reach out and allow friends and family to minister on our behalf can lead to loneliness, despair, and failure. We were not made to shoulder our burdens alone. By no means did my family walk down the path with Chris without the support of many sincere and generous people.

Kindness and Generosity

These words from First Timothy best describe the many acts of kindness and generosity we received during and after Chris's illness and death. "Command them to do good, to be rich in good deeds, and to be generous and willing to share. In this way they will lay up treasure for themselves as a firm foundation for the coming age, so that they may take hold of this life that is truly life" (1 Timothy 6:18–19).

Timothy reminds us that all we have comes from God. Wealth and abundance comes with great responsibility. The church at Ephesus was encouraged to give of their riches for the glory of God. When you help someone with your finances, time, or talents, you are in essence giving glory to God. In Jesus Christ we have much to be thankful for. We are also called to be rich in our good deeds toward others. When we willingly share and do acts of service, we have unlocked one of the greatest secrets for living a fruitful, abundant life. Fox Valley Presbyterian Church understood and not only gave of their finances but performed other acts of generosity on our behalf also.

Let Me Count the Ways

We received financial assistance during Chris's illness and after her death. When I went back to school in pursuit of my undergraduate and graduate studies, financial aid would come to us from different sources. Sometimes, there would be checks in the mail or cash sent in cards or just handed to us. Those finances always seemed to come just at the time we needed it the most. Many friends went with Jan down to Children's Memorial Hospital in Chicago when Chris had to undergo tests. Others offered their babysitting services during our many day trips to the hospital.

Clean and White/Dining Delights

The week Chris's leukemia was diagnosed, members of Jan's book study group at church came to our home while we were at the hospital with her. They did a thorough spring cleaning of our entire house, washing windows, floors, bedding, and curtains. Every time Chris had to be in the hospital for a period of time, our faithful church members would bring dinners for our entire family. During the last month of Chris's life, we had more than thirty meals brought to our home. Some would bring flowers, treats, or gifts for Connie and Diane as well.

Constant Blessings

The church helped me secure a student loan my last year in seminary. They defrayed the cost of Jan's hospital bill when she had surgery while I was in school. While I was in seminary, the church literally made one Christmas possible for our children. They even furnished a turkey and ham for our festive holiday dinner. Finally, our dental and doctor bills were taken care of when I was in school. Besides these and other acts of kindness, others supported us with encouragement, cards, prayers and phone calls.

Finally, Answers

A few weeks after Chris passed away, we received the answers we had all been looking for. Up to the time of Chris's death, the staff at Children's Memorial Hospital could not provide a medical explanation for why Chris died. Chris's autopsy report revealed that her leukemia had metastasized to another form of cancer and attacked her vital organs. At the time there were no other cases like hers in the medical journals. We were also told that Chris was the first child with ALL (Acute Lymphocytic Leukemia) to metastasize and also to recover from Pneumocystis Carnii (a form of pneumonia). My first reaction was to wonder what the odds had been of Chris getting leukemia in the first place, and what the odds had been that her original diagnosis would turn into another form of cancer. For a brief moment I was exasperated over the autopsy report, thinking of how her death was so unfair. However, God's grace and mercy replaced my frustration with peace and contentment.

Memory Like a Steal Trap

Friends, try as we might, the reality is that we cannot delete God's memory. He knows all. Jan and I came to depend on the fact that God would not be absentminded about His promises to us. We continually stepped out in faith, knowing He would not forget our needs no matter what we were going through. This is great life-changing news for all those who have put their trust in Jesus! Joel reminds us, "Do not be afraid, O land, be glad and rejoice. Surely the Lord has done great things" (Joel 2:21).

Setting Us Free

God doesn't promise us a perpetual rose garden. He doesn't promise that all followers of Jesus will prosper. On this side of heaven we will attend funerals and experience sorrow, pain, and discouragement sandwiched in between some joy and accomplishment. However, Jesus assures us that we can rise above our circumstances. He has great things in store for those who trust and follow Him! *Remember—Jesus, the giver of life, frees us from consuming strife.*

Thank You, Fox Valley

We were blessed by a church that was willing to be used by God during our trials and tribulations and to celebrate with us at my ordination. God used Fox Valley Presbyterian Church to help fulfill His purpose for our lives and ministry. We were and still are eternally appreciative of how God used this church as an instrument of grace in our lives.

Embracing God's promises is an act of faith.

"Brother Love's Traveling Salvation Show"
Words by: Neil Diamond
(Some lyrics paraphrased)

It was a smoldering late summer night with leaves drooping.
You could smell the sweet aroma of the grass.

Traveling along approaching the town
You could hear the gospel sound.
There in a worn tent, in the clearing
The gospel team was singing to us.

Young and old go to the traveling gospel show
Because everybody has heard and no one is left behind
The salvation show is in town.

In an instant silence fills the room, it's like
You could almost hear the drops of perspiration roll down your face.
Just as the preacher enters
Every eye is fixed on his presence.
All ears are tuned on him.
He starts out quietly like a tremor.
Then he roars and part of the valley trembles.
The preacher shouts when your brother is in trouble
You need to extend one of your two hands to him.
That is why you have them.

And when your heart aches
You must extend your other hand to him.
Then you are to lift your hands to the Lord
Because that is what He is waiting for you to do.

Place your hand in His and He will be with you
Each step of the way so you won't wander.

CHAPTER FOURTEEN

"Salvation Show"

My Call

It took us several months after Chris's death to get back into some kind of a normal lifestyle. During this time I sensed that God was calling me into some form of Christian ministry. We took my nudging to our Christian friends in prayer, seeking confirmation and direction. In the fall after Chris died, God seemed to be leading me into taking a few Bible courses at Moody Bible Institute to test my calling. I attended Moody at night while working full time at Jewel. I really enjoyed my courses at Moody. One of my professors was really affirming and encouraged my call. All the confirmation I had received at this point leaned toward pursuing the ordination process for pastoral ministry. Brother Carr's journey toward the Lord's salvation show was about to become a reality.

You've Got to Be Kidding Me!

I met with my pastor the Reverend Tom Estes for lunch and advice. We talked about ministry in general. I shared with him my desire and sense of call to church ministry. After lunch Pastor Estes drove me home. It was in my driveway sitting in his car that my life began taking on a whole new meaning. I posed a direct question to Pastor Estes and asked what steps I would need to take to become an ordained Presbyterian pastor. He told me I would have to first finish my undergraduate program and then obtain a Master of Divinity degree at an accredited seminary. The more he shared about my requirements, the more apprehensive I became. I just stared at my home in bewilderment, thinking about a mortgage, a wife, three children, and my full-time job. Panic had officially set in as I thought to myself, You have got to be kidding! How can I possibly do this? Suddenly my feet weren't only cold, but ice cold! I must admit I was numb with fear and anxiety about the unknown.

No Turning Back

Jan and I gathered all the information given to us and lifted it up in prayer. We counted the cost in terms of what our family had recently gone through. In less than one year, we lost a daughter, which created a tremendous upheaval in our lives, and gained a son. Quitting my full-time job to complete my undergraduate program and then seminary would require a great sacrifice involving the whole family. Both Jan and I knew God's hand was on my calling into pastoral ministry. One thing we had learned during the three years with Chris was the importance of knowing and doing God's will in Christ no matter what the price. *There will come a time when God calls us to put our prayers into action.*

Putting It on the Line

Once again we came to the feet of our Lord Jesus, seeking His courage, strength, counsel, direction, and will. We had learned a very important lesson along the way.

We stepped out in faith and said, "Yes, Lord . . . If this is Your will for us, then we are in." We placed our trust in the fact that Jesus would provide for our needs every step along the way. *God's way is always the best way.*

Back to School

God led me to Judson College in Elgin, Illinois. It was perfect for me, because I wanted to major in religion. Judson offered a comprehensive degree program in religion and philosophy. I enrolled as a full-time student at Judson College in the fall of 1978. I could not work for Jewel as a meat cutter part time, so I had to quit my job as market manager and find part-time work elsewhere. I worked part time at grocery stores, a concrete plant, and doing security. It certainly was not easy, balancing my academics with work and family responsibilities, but God richly blessed us. He truly provided a way when at times it appeared there was no way. I graduated from Judson College in 1980 and entered The Church of the Brethren Seminary in the fall of that year.

Let the Good Times Roll

Throughout my time in college and seminary we always managed to go on a vacation during spring breaks. I firmly believe this was because we always honored our financial tithe to the church. When God called me to leave Jewel and attend school full time, we never relinquished our original tithe. We maintained that pledge amount even when our earnings were considerably less. God just blessed our faithfulness in giving.

Blessings Beyond Measure

In the OT the storehouse was a place in the temple where grain was stored that the people had given for tithes. The people in Malachi's day had disobeyed God by not offering their tithes and offerings to the Almighty. Consider this: if we are not faithful to God in our giving, we rob not only God but also ourselves of His blessings and grace. The purpose of tithing (10 percent of our income) is not to see what we can get from God. Tithing expresses our love and faith in God. God promises to bless our sincere faithfulness in our giving. Philippians 4:10–19 confirms this.

Malachi 3:10 makes one of the most extraordinary claims in the Bible. "Test Me in this, says the Lord Almighty, and see if I will not throw open the floodgates of Heaven and pour out so much blessing that you won't have enough room for it." Malachi was not talking about a theology of prosperity. It's not about playing Let's Make a Deal with God or trying to buy or bribe Him. The Psalmist wrote, "Taste and see that the Lord is good; blessed is the man who takes refuge in Him" (Psalm 34:8). Both of these verses boldly challenge us to prove, test, taste, and see that our Lord is good, kind, and generous. As we turn to God in our daily obedience and trust Him with everything, even our finances, we see just how wonderful and giving God truly is!

Taste the Goodness of God

I submit Malachi's and David's challenges to all those reading this book. Test God for yourself and see if He is good, kind, and faithful. If you put your heart in God's hand, you will discover a remarkable truth. He will never, ever let you down! Some say, "Prove to me that God exists, prove to me that God still does miracles today, prove to me the Bible is God's revelation, prove to me Jesus died and was resurrected, and prove to me that God knows even the number of hairs on my head." If you want this kind of proof, then the first thing you must do is test His goodness and faithfulness. You do so by honoring and loving Him with all your heart. This includes obeying and trusting Him with your life and finances. When you do all these things, you will be absolutely astounded at how He will work in your life in ways beyond human expectations.

The Choices We Make

Throughout our lives we are confronted with a series of choices. When we choose to follow God, we find peace, direction, purpose, fulfillment, and salvation. When we simply choose to follow our natural inclinations, we come to realize that something is missing in life. We learn the valuable truth that we cannot solve all our problems by reading a how-to-be-successful book, or picking the brains of the most intelligent people on this earth in search of answers to the mysteries of life. We all need divine intervention at some point, for that is the way God has wired us. *However, the longer you tune God out of your life, the harder it becomes to tune Him in.*

Shame on You, Denny

Now, there were those who thought that going back to school was the wrong decision for me. Perhaps I was putting God to a foolish test. Some thought I was sacrificing too much and asking too much of my family, placing many hardships upon them so I could finish my education in preparation for ordination. The truth was that we had counted the cost of making a complete life change. We also knew my eventual ordination was God's will. Our confidence rested on the providence of God and in no one else. We stood on the Word of God, confident that He would supply all our needs in Christ Jesus. God always gave us just enough to get by. He wanted us to be totally, completely sold out and dependent on Jesus, and we were. Jan and I believed that if God could strengthen and sustain us during Chris's illness and death, He could see us through anything.

There Must Be Something Seriously Wrong with Jan and

Denny

Working various part-time jobs did not compensate for a reduction of our earnings. We prayed about our financial tithe to the church. Should we adjust it according to our current income? After a time of prayer, we were led to maintain the pledge we had made while I was working full time at Jewel. One year our income was below the poverty level. My father-in-law was an accountant who also filed our income taxes. Our earnings stunned him. He just could not grasp why we were giving so much to the church when we were in financial poverty. It was a challenge, to say the least, to try to convince my father-in-law that everything was okay and we were not crazy! We stood firm and obeyed the Word and continued our tithe offering, much to my father-in-law's grave concern and against his financial advice.

The Choicest Meats

The astounding thing about our year of living at the poverty level was that we dined on the finest cuts of beef three days a week. You might be thinking, How could this be? Shortly before the beginning of that year, a food store I worked for had problems with its fresh-meat case. The cuts of meat would lose eye appeal. So approximately every three days or so we would box perfectly good meat displayed in the meat counter and store it in the holding freezer. We accumulated a number of boxes full of different kinds of steaks and beef roasts. When the store closed, the manager sold all those boxes in the freezer to me for one hundred dollars!

A Feast for Sure

Consider what was going on here. I was a full-time student with a mortgage, a wife, three children, and earnings below the poverty level for a whole year. Yet we were giving a financial offering to a church that we could not possibly afford from a human perspective. We were eating filet mignon, New York strips, Porterhouse, T-bone, sirloin steaks, and other choice beef roasts three days a week for that whole impoverished year. We had tasted and seen that the Lord was good once again. He opened the gates of heaven and poured out more unusual blessings upon us beyond our wildest dreams. An important lesson was once again confirmed to us. We will never be able to totally understand the fullness of God's storehouse of blessings.

Three and Out

My third year in seminary finally arrived. It had been an odyssey of study, work, and trying to pay the bills. God had been faithful every step along our journey. There were many frustrating times for sure. However, we could finally see that light at the end of the tunnel. My goal for the sake of the family was to finish the Master of Divinity program in three years. It was my conviction to do so because I did not want my family to endure any more hardship than necessary. They had already dealt with so much. The emotional loss of Chris, combined with a new baby and my going back to school, created a great deal of stress for all.

What's on First, Who's on Second?

It seems like God kept us living on the edge. I firmly believe the challenges He placed before us were for the purpose of preparing and testing us to depend totally upon Him for all things. My final year at McCormick Theological Seminary in Chicago was filled with research papers, finals, and investigating potential churches for ministry and preparation for ordination exams. Because of my class schedule, I spent Monday through Thursday staying at my in-laws' home in Berwyn, Illinois.

On the Go

Mid-Thursday morning after my last class, I would drive home to Saint Charles to spend the weekends with my family. Then it was working at my part-time jobs, term papers or studying for exams, and so on. That year I worked twenty hours a week cutting meat at a local food chain. On Sundays I was involved in an internship (field education) program. In the evening I did youth ministry at the same church. God provided the income, but I was beginning to run on empty. I found myself being pulled in many different directions. My hectic schedule put some stress not only on me, but more important, on my family. Jan had been working part time plus trying to keep the family organized.

The Hulk

I would arrive home at noon on Thursdays. My son, David, now five, and I had begun a new tradition. After lunch we would play *The Incredible Hulk*. One Thursday I arrived home at my usual time and David was eagerly waiting for me, all excited and ready to play Hulk (he was the Hulk and I was the bad guy). I was anxious and stressed about meeting some academic deadlines. I had to write a major term paper plus work thirty hours over the weekend. I thought that the pressure of these obligations would require every spare moment available. I told David we couldn't play because I was just too busy with other things that needed to get done. The look on my son's face would have broken your heart. After lunch as I was planning my project, God would not let me off the hook.

Priorities

The Holy Spirit just convicted my heart to set aside my hectic schedule and play with my son. David was far more important than any term paper or job responsibility. I was obedient to the Spirit's conviction. We played and had a great time. I did not think or even worry about that paper. I was too busy being the "bad guy." It felt good and right because God had helped put my priorities in order.

I Would Do It All Over Again

The writer of Ecclesiastes wrote, "There is a time for everything, and a season for every activity under Heaven: a time to be born and a time to die, a time to plant and a time to uproot, a time to kill and a time to heal, a time to tear down and a time to build, a time to weep and a time to laugh, a time to mourn and a time to dance, a time to scatter stones and a time to gather them" (Ecclesiastes 3:1-5). The writer of these verses reminds us that God is not only in control but has a purpose for our lives. He balances all facets of life, birth, death, sorrow, joy, work, play, mourning, celebrating, planting, and harvest. I believe the key to finding balance in our own lives lies in understanding that what we experience is guided by God's perfect timing. When I decided to play with David instead of lamenting that I just didn't have the time, God blessed our playing together and the completion of my paper because I accepted His perfect timing and not mine.

The Character of God

The seven-part fulfillment of God's revelation spoken into Jan's heart in 1976 is so true of His character. At the time we didn't get it. However, looking back at the seven promises God had given Jan, they only confirm how loving, caring, merciful, all knowing, and just our mighty God is. God knows and acts according to what is best for all those who seek to follow the ways of the Lord. Yes, God's timing and plans are always perfect.

I've Never Been So Happy in My Whole Life!

I will never forget my last day in seminary. It was a cool but crystal-clear Chicago spring day. I had just completed my final exam and handed it in, knowing that I had done well. As I floated down that flight of stairs at McCormick Theological Seminary, I was euphoric. A sense of relief at "mission accomplished" overwhelmed me. I had successfully passed my ordination requirement exams, and a church was waiting to call me to be their pastor. All the trials, heartaches, frustrations, challenges, and sacrifices of the past few years flashed through my mind. It was done, finished, over! I walked to my car with briefcase in hand, celebrating, just overwhelmed with joy and a sense of accomplishment. God had taught us so much in terms of how to trust, persevere, and cling to Jesus. Looking back on those days, I can honestly say that without direction from God's Word, prayer, and Jesus' supernatural intervention, there was absolutely no way we could have achieved our goal. *When you read the Bible, pray, and follow Jesus' ways, the Holy Spirit will guide your days.*

A New Chapter Begins

Graduation and all the requirements for ordination in the Presbyterian denomination were now behind us. It was time to pack up the kids and get the Carrs' salvation show on the road. This move came with mixed emotions. We were leaving our first home with all the memories and the moments we had shared with Chris. We were leaving our friends who had supported us through the joys and the heartbreaks. We were leaving our home church that had supported and encouraged us beyond what we could have possibly imagined or hoped for. But it was time to leave. We put our home on the market, and off we went. I was ordained in August 1983 at our home church, Fox Valley Presbyterian, and accepted a call to pastor a Presbyterian Church in Piper City, Illinois.

God Is So Good

Within weeks of settling in our new home and adjusting to my calling, our house in Saint Charles sold. I truly believe one cannot out give God. Permit me to recap what God had done for us in our journey toward ordination with a family consisting of a husband, wife, three children, and a mortgage. We left Saint Charles and within a few short weeks our home was sold. We did not carry over a single debt, including fees for college and seminary. God even provided a new car and furniture for our home in Piper City. We even had a surplus to start a savings account. How is that for God meeting our needs "according to His glorious riches in Christ Jesus" (Philippians 4:19)?

Without a Doubt

As Lamentations so appropriately reads, "The Lord is good to those whose hope is in Him, to the one who seeks Him" (Lamentations 3:25). The writer tells us that God is always faithful to those who seek Him first. We constantly lifted our burdens up to the Lord Jesus and trusted His faithfulness in our times of fear. He would always come through, give us hope, and deliver us from our problems. It may sound simplistic, but it was true in our case. *By focusing on God's faithfulness in the past, we can count on God's faithfulness in the present.*

Prophecies Fulfilled

In chapter 8 I shared how God sent Jan a love letter (prophecy) about coming events that would be fulfilled in our lives. Jan received this revelation from God in 1976 at Camp Timberlee. The revelation consisted of seven coming events. 1) Chris would have a new birth; 2) Jan would become pregnant; 3) the baby would be a son (David was born in 1977); 4) God gave Jan the baby's name and she kept it hidden in her heart until I confirmed the name David; 5) our finances would change (I left Jewel to work part time jobs); 6. I would have a job change (from meat cutter to pastor); and 7. we would have a new home (we moved to Piper City in 1983). Consider this: God placed in Jan's heart seven coming events that were fulfilled in seven years! Would you say they were mere coincidences or were they God's incidences? You may draw your own conclusions. However, I would be hard pressed to leave what God had revealed to mere chance.

An Amazing Number

The number seven is used hundreds of times throughout the sixty-six books of the Bible, from the first book, Genesis, to the last book, Revelation. The number seven in Scripture symbolizes *completeness* or *perfection.* God never does anything by chance, nor does He play mind games or attempt to trick us. The Holy Spirit will never contradict the Word of God. The Bible tells us that when Jesus ascended into heaven, His physical presence left the earth, but Jesus promised to send the Holy Spirit (the Spirit of truth) so that his Spiritual presence would dwell within the believer. The Holy Spirit is in every believer today. The question is, Do we call upon His power source in our lives?

What More Can Be Said?

There are times when God speaks to us in dramatic, powerful ways, when we experience divine fireworks. There are times when God speaks to us in a still, quiet voice. My point is that He speaks to us, using whatever means necessary according to His Word, to get our attention and fulfill His purposes.

Following God

Following God often comes with a cost. In Genesis we read, "The Lord had said to Abram, Leave your country, your people and your father's household and go to the land I will show you. I will make you into a great nation and I will bless you; I will make your name great, and you will be a blessing. I will bless those who bless you and whoever curses you I will curse" (Genesis 12:1-3). When God called Abram (Abraham) in Ur of the Chaldees, he moved out in faith. Abraham remained in Haran until the death of his father. God established a covenant with Abraham because of his obedience. God's promise consisted of four parts: 1) Abraham would be a great nation; 2) God would bless him; 3) God would make his name great; 4) Abraham would be a blessing to all. However, there was one condition behind these promises. God wanted Abraham to do what He told him to do. That meant Abraham was to leave his home, familiar surroundings, and friends, and move to a new, foreign land. God blessed Abraham because He obeyed.

You'd Better Move On

Abraham just packed up his family, some possessions, camels, and donkeys, and off he went to a foreign land. Remember, God did not supply Abraham with a GPS to tell him which route to take. He trusted God for directions. When Abraham left, turning back was not an option as far as he was concerned.

The Plan

God said it, and that was enough for him. Abraham did not complain, debate, hesitate, or procrastinate. He took God at His word, and depended on His promise of blessings and a better future. God knew what was around the corner of Abraham's life, and he simply trusted in God's plan for him and his household.

Follow the Leader

Like Abraham we were trying to follow the Lord. Yes, we made our share of mistakes along the way. Making a commitment to follow the Lord is often not easy. It comes with many challenges. We sought the Lord's leading even when we were clueless and His plan was not on our radar screen. There were times when we wanted our prayers answered from our human perspective instead of God's perspective. However, at the end of the day our desire was to be obedient to the Holy Spirit's nudges regardless of the outcome. *With Jesus we have everything, but without Him we have nothing.*

Salvation Show

Preaching and proclaiming the inspired Word of God is fundamental in the Christian faith. Paul in the book of Romans 10:13 said, "For everyone who calls on the name of the Lord will be saved." The church of Jesus Christ needs to major in the basics of biblical truth. Perhaps as Christians we spend too much time debating or protecting what makes our denomination distinct from other denominations. Some actually believe their church is the only true church. However, that is simply not true, according to the Word of God. What makes us one in the Spirit is Jesus Christ and no other. My prayer is that all believers and the church at large will concentrate on the fundamentals or the basics of the faith. They are 1) to *believe* Jesus died on the cross, paid the price for our sins, and was resurrected, so that all who believe in Him will also have eternal life in heaven; 2) to *repent*, confess your sins, and turn away from the old sinful self and turn to Jesus for forgiveness and grace; 3) to *trust* you can do all things in Christ. He is the Way, the Truth, and the Life. No one comes to the Father except through Him (John 14:6). This is the gospel message for which we should rejoice and be unified.

We become God's treasured possession when we accept Jesus' resurrection.

"Moments to Remember"
Words by: Robert Allen and Al Stillman
(Some lyrics paraphrased)

From the first of the year to the last month we have those unforgettable memories.
All those peaceful walks, the fun times
We came close to winning the dance prize
We will never forget those memories.

As the seasons come and go
And the present becomes the past
All the good times we shared together will
Be remembered.

When the days and nights pass by
We discover time has drawn us apart.
We will never forget those memories.

Those nights at the drive-in the movies we didn't watch are lasting memories.
When the days and nights pass by
We discover time has drawn us apart
We will never forget those memories.

CHAPTER FIFTEEN

"Moments to Remember"

Chris Revealed

Chris's voice has been silenced by death. Therefore, the purpose of this chapter is to give the reader a personal glimpse of Chris—what was in her heart, some of her thoughts, and how she reacted to some of the afflictions that became so much a part of her life. Chris's words come from her personal journals, other items, and input from family, friends, and others who knew her or heard her story.

Flies in the Salad

The intent of this chapter and *Time After Time* is not to put Chris on some pedestal but rather to give the reader a clearer understanding of who she really was in life. We had no illusions. Like any child her age Chris had her share of flaws. She was, at times, a pint-sized sinner.

Just a Kid

Chris did not have a halo hanging over her head. In many ways she was like any other ordinary kid growing up. She was a typical older sister. She could be a real intimidating thorn in her younger sisters' sides. For example, her sisters were not allowed in her room without her permission. Chris even went as far as using the doorway leading into her room as the boundary line. Connie and Diane couldn't cross that line without her permission. Chris, her sisters, and some of their friends (the Seidel girls) would play doctor. Chris was the doctor, and Nancy (her best friend) was the nurse. Connie, Diane, and Michele and Heather Seidel would be the patients at the doctor's office. They had to follow Chris's script almost to the letter. Improvising by the patients was not tolerated. It was either Chris's way or no way.

The Bottom Line

I believe Chris's time at play, to a great extent, was her escape from the harsh realities that surrounded her. Time and disease would not permit her to remain in a make-believe world for very long. Yes, in many ways Chris was ordinary, but we could not deny that she was also very special. Most of the children we encountered with terminal illnesses were special. We used to say Chris was ten going on thirty. How she looked at life and conducted herself with all her physical and psychological traumas was truly inspiring. There are moments when we look back and marvel at how she handled what was on her plate. The bottom line for Chris was faith in her Jesus. Perhaps this passage from John best defines Chris's relationship with her Lord. "Then Jesus declared, "I am the bread of life. He who comes to Me will never go hungry, and he who believes in Me will never be thirsty" (John 6:35).

Are You Hungry or Thirsty?

Jesus made a bold claim that literally sustained Chris in life and death. Jesus said He could satisfy our spiritual hunger and thirst like no other. Jesus gives life and nourishes all who ask Him into their hearts. Chris had this strong, quiet faith, knowing Jesus would sustain her not only in this life but also in the resurrection to eternal life. Chris had a daily hunger and thirst for Jesus, the "bread of life."

I sincerely believe she would want that for every person reading this book. Life—past present, and future—can be sweet for those who receive and trust Jesus as Lord and Savior. He is sufficient for every person under any circumstance. *Jesus can mend a wounded heart.*

A Daughter Never Forgotten

The song "Moments to Remember" reminds me of Chris's short life with us. Even though Chris was with us for only a season, the effect she had on friends, acquaintances, and her family are still felt today. We can all recall throwing stones in the water while we were growing up. We would watch as that stone hit the water and created a rippling effect. That was how Chris's life touched those who knew her. The rippling effect of her brief life is still evident today. Seasons come and go, and the good times we used to share come back to us as the years go by. Those memories we have of Chris are just as strong today and in some ways stronger in Jan and me than ever before.

The Folder

Most of us can remember having those special folders when we were in school. In them we kept our homework assignments and things that were important to us. On the cover of our folders we would often write things that we valued and thought were significant. For some it was the name of a boyfriend, girlfriend, or the latest sayings. No matter what we wrote, those words, names, and phrases meant a great deal to us. In a sense what we had written down on our folders helped define us.

Chris's Words

The following is a list of single words or mini-phrases we found on the outside of Chris's fifth-grade school folder. Some of them describe a typical kid at ten, but most reveal a more serious side of Chris. They represented what she valued and affirmed as important and lasting in her life. Below each word or phrase on her folder was a swirling line to highlight what she had written.

Chris Carr
Jesus
Good
Live forever
Life is great
Peace
Joy
Love
Great
Life is to Live
Nice
I'm great

Inside Chris's folder we found some of her homework, art projects, and pictures of horses, her favorite animals. She also had a puzzle with the words "and the child grew" based on Luke 2:39–40. It showed Mary and Jesus as a boy. The title of the puzzle was "Mary and the Boy Jesus."

Little Things Mean a Lot

Sometimes we think it's the big things in a person's life that determine what they believe, proclaim, value, prioritize, spend their money on, and so on. As I was going through Chris's personal belongings, a number of her possessions caught my attention. Chris surrounded herself with things pertaining to the faith. She was an avid reader. Her teacher once said you could put Chris in a rocking chair all day long reading a book and she would be content. All of her bookmarks had a faith component to them. For example:

Title: "Just for Today"

"Lord for tomorrow and its needs I do not pray; Keep me, my God, from stain of sin, just for today. Now set a seal upon my lips, for this I pray; Keep me from wrong or idle words, Just for today. Let me be slow to do my will, Prompt to obey, And keep me, guide me, use me, Lord, Just for today."

The following bookmark Chris used was very fitting for her life.

Title: "What God Hath Promised:"

"God hath not promised Skies always blue, Flower-strewn pathways All our lives thro'; God hath not promised Sun without rain, Joy without sorrow, Peace without pain. God hath not promised We shall not know Toil or temptation, Trouble and woe; He hath not told us We shall not bear many a burden, Many a care. But God hath promised Strength for the day, Rest for the laborer, Light for the weary, grace for the trials, Help from above, Unfailing sympathy, Undying love." Selected (author unknown)

Chris's Journals

I have collected some of Chris's works and believe they will help the reader in some way to know what influenced her heart and mind. Once again we marveled that the overwhelming majority of her personal possessions were things that spoke of her faith. They are testimonies to us some thirty-plus years later. I hope in some fashion that her personal items will be a witness to you as well. As I have mentioned, Chris, like her mom, kept a daily journal. The following are some of Chris's thoughts in her own words.

Chris Interpreted the 23rd Psalm

The Lord is my Shepherd and I am his sheep!
> Because the Lord is my shepherd, I have everything I
> need!
> He lets me rest in the meadow grass and leads me beside
> the quiet streams.
> He restores my failing health. He helps me do what honors
> him most.
> Even when walking through the dark valley of death
> I will not be afraid, for you are close beside me guarding,
> guiding all the way.
> You provided delicious food for me in the presence of my
> enemies.
> You have welcomed me as your guest, blessings overflow!
> Your goodness and unfailing kindness shall be with me
> All my life, and afterwards I will live with you forever in
> your home.

The following are other entries in Chris's journal.

The Morning Bright

> "The morning bright with rosy light hath waked me from
> my sleep;
> Father, thine own great love alone Thy little one doth
> keep."

"Tender Jesus Meek and Mild"

> Tender Jesus, Meek and Mild

Look on me, thy little child
Help me, if it be Thy will
To recover from all ill."

Ah, dearest Jesus, Holy Child

"Ah, dearest Jesus, holy child,
Make thee a bed, soft and undefiled,
Within my heart, that it may be
A quiet chamber kept for thee."

Lord Jesus, Bless the pastor's word

"Lord Jesus, bless the pastor's word upon
my heart. I pray that after all is
said and heard I gladly may obey."

Be Near Me, Lord Jesus

"Be near me, Lord Jesus,
I ask Thee to stay close by me forever.
And love me I pray.
Bless all the dear children in Thy
Tender care; and take us to Heaven
To live with Thee there.
Come, Lord Jesus
Come, Lord Jesus
Be our guest,
And let thy gifts
To us be blest."

Our Hands We Fold

"Our hands we fold, our heads we bow,
For food and drink we thank Thee now."

Father, Bless Our School Today

"Father bless our school today
Father bless our school today
Be in all we do or say, be in every song we sing;
Every prayer to Thee we bring.
Oh, give thanks unto the Lord
Oh, give thanks unto the Lord
For He is good;
For His mercy endureth."

Dear God, My Heavenly Father

"Dear God, my heavenly Father,
Bless me at school today,
And help me learn my lessons;
In Jesus name I pray."

Savior, Use the Gift I Lay

"Savior, use the gift I lay
Humbly at Thy feet today;
May it bring some child to Thee,
There to live eternally."

Chris's Story

The following is a story Chris wrote.

My Life—Unedited

My name is Christine Carr. I'm 8 years old. I have a very rare disease called leukemia. It is a very dangerous disease. Leukemia is a disease of the blood. It used to be a killing disease. Now people have come up with extensive research, they have controlled it. I had it for 4 months and I got a pneumonia called pneumocystics carnii. It almost killed me. Then that is when my mom and dad really turned to the Lord. And all of us changed. I changed, my sisters changed, and mom and dad changed too. A little while ago I had two painful shots called a bone marrow and 3 lps' and they really hurt and boy did the Lord really take the pain in those shots because I would usually cry for them but I didn't.

The End

A Doctor's Poem

This poem was written by one of the doctors who attended Chris during one of her hospital stays.

Title: "For Chris"

Silliness
Not part of Chris
So many answers
For just a thimble of years
No tears
Very grown
A seedling prematurely sown

Inside out

> Accessible to all
> *Gentle call*
>
> *I like you*
> *Want you to know*
> *You're very soft*
> *Like a marshmallow*

Friends Remember

We asked some of our friends who were very close to our family during Chris's illness to share some of their thoughts.

Sandy Remembers

What I remember is a girl who still had joy and a zest for life. A girl who giggled and loved. A girl who asked Jesus to help her with the pain of those horrible tests. A girl who loved God even in the midst of her disease. I am reminded of Hannah, who gave her son to the Lord, literally. Now as Christians we know they belong to God. We give them to God but, whether consciously or unconsciously, we feel we can take them back if necessary. God called Denny and Jan to give Chris to Him permanently. For a mom who doesn't want her grown kids more than ten miles away, it is impossible for me to fully imagine the sacrifice you made. Yet this we do know. God calls us to give our children to Him for Him and to use, as He will for His eternal glory. God used Chris for His glory while she was with us. I think we will never know how many came to Christ because of Chris. The real miracle is that He continues to use her life and her death for His glory and to bring people to Him. How many parties have there been with the angels in heaven for one who has come to Jesus because of Chris's life?

Praise God for her life with us and for her life dancing in the streets of heaven with Jesus.

Love, Sandy Petrille

Beth Remembers

Looking back it is fascinating to see how God drew us together at that particular time in our lives. Dave and I were the newest in the area—and to Fox Valley Presbyterian Church—and to what became the quartet of families who shared lives with each other—sharing tears, laughter, confusion, rejoicing, insights, celebrations, losses, and best of all a continual deepening in our faith, joy, and trust in our Lord. When Chris left us and went to be with Jesus, it was the first time I had ever dealt with death other than my grandparents. Now I see I really ran from my own feelings and kept myself quite busy . . . like not attending the funeral service by offering to stay at the house to set up for the people arriving later. Hmmmm . . . Just did not know how to risk letting my feelings show, or even recognize how deeply I did "feel." I do remember while driving downstate to a Presbyterian Women's meeting being amazed at how the world went on about its business. The sun still shone, people were still grumpy, or silly, or happy . . . Didn't they know that we had lost our Chrissy?

Beth Luther

Carol Remembers

Jan and I never hesitated watching each other's children. Their girls were (and are) an extension to our family, so when Chris became ill, it was only natural: I wanted and needed to help out in any way I could. The girls were quite young when Chris got sick and really didn't understand the severity of leukemia. But as time marched on, Chris's extended hospital stays, chemo, and other treatments performed began to show their physical effects on her body. The girls could see the changes but as only children can do; they looked beyond and treated Chris as always, allowing her to join in play any way she could. Even if for only a few moments at a time Chris would play as a "little girl" with her sisters and friends. Chris being the oldest was a typical first child—mature, intelligent, methodical with strong leadership skills—but was beyond her ten years when it came to her faith in Jesus and her unwonted spirit. As I watched Chris, I came to a better understanding of what Matthew 18:3-4 meant, when Jesus said, "I tell you the truth, unless you change and become like little children, you will never enter the kingdom of Heaven. Therefore, whoever humbles himself like this child is the greatest in the kingdom of Heaven." Even in Chris's darkest moments, she recognized God's presence and power. Chris had many favorite Psalms, but for me, the one that I feel describes her walk with the Lord is Psalm 27. Our family's lives have been forever enriched by the Lord allowing us the privilege of walking alongside Chris and her family. We may not always understand God's ways, but through faith in His son Jesus Christ we can live a life of victory even through tragedy. Our lives have been woven together like a fine tapestry. This was not of our doing but God's. The story is an account of Chris's journey and how her faith and courage were an inspiration for all of us. Although she only had ten and a half years on earth, the impact she had on our lives will live with us forever. Chris's hope was to share her faith so others could receive God's most precious gift. John 3:16 says, "For God so loved the world that He gave His one and only Son. That whoever believes in Him shall not perish but have eternal life."

Thanks to you, Chris, and your family for leading us to the cross!

Carol Seidel

A Family Remembers

The following are thoughts from Chris's uncle, sisters, brother, and mother.

Uncle Steve Remembers

She never moved large crowds of people through spiritual awaking,

She never had written a book highlighting the spirit filled life,

Nor did she put pen to paper, with deep spiritual truths leading to profound ministry.

What she did do is show Christ in her death, which has everlasting impact.

I remember the night my brother called me to tell of the disease his daughter had invading her body.

A disease which would, one day, consume her life. Chris was diagnosed with leukemia. I felt so much anger and cursed a God whom I didn't believe existed. How does one curse that which does not exist?

The few years Chris struggled with her illness created a monumental impact upon my life. Not profound because of the disease; rather it was profound because of how Chris lived out the last two years of her life.

The last time I saw Chris alive, she was hooked up to a vast array of equipment.

It looked like something from a science fiction lab with all the tubes of liquid invading her body.

Her face was gray and her eyes were aged beyond her years.

The machines were forcing life into a body, which could no longer sustain itself.

As I walked into that room, there was a countenance in her eyes that was angelic.

There was a peace in her eyes even though she was being overtaken by death.

As I walked into the room, she gave me a weak but distinctive smile.

I could not understand the smile in the midst of her tragedy. However, because of her peace in the circumstance she was in, I came to have a desire to have what she had.

Chris, by her silent testimony, was used by God to bring me to faith in Jesus Christ.

I have thought often about Chris and her impact on many people.

I am just one of many where God used Chris to be a silent witness of His glory.

I know one day I will see Chris again, and I know God has put Chris in charge of much in His kingdom."

Steve Carr

Connie Remembers

"On the night Chris died, I really don't remember Mom or Dad coming and telling me.

I remember Diane, Mom, Dad, and myself all sleeping together that night in my mom and dad's room.

I did not really sleep that night, but felt numb and almost in a kind of shock of it all, like it was a bad dream or something.

Then I felt this pit of sadness.

I was sad because I never got the chance to tell Chris I loved her or give her one last hug or kiss.

Did she really know how much I loved and missed her?

I knew she was in heaven, but I wanted my big sister to stay with us.

Then I just shut down.

I did not want to think about not being able to see her again.

I just didn't want to think about it. Those were was some of my feelings about the night Chris died.

Connie (Carr) Baker

Diane Remembers

The details of the night my sister died are blurry, but the feelings I can remember like it was yesterday. I remember my parents telling us Chrissy had died and we all went to sleep together in their bed. I felt so very restless, hopeless, and sad. I wanted to fall asleep to escape the painful reality, but couldn't. Even a child understands that when someone dies on this earth, they are not coming back. I was so sad because I did not get to say good-bye to her. I just wished I could tell her all those things you wish you could tell someone if you knew you would never see them again. I remember thinking, How can we go on without crying constantly? Does she know how much I love her? How do we live now? I had a pit in my stomach of deep sadness, with no hope of it ever going away. Now that I am an adult, sometimes I just want to go back in time and hold that baby girl and tell her, "It will be okay; you'll see. God will yet fill your mouth with laughter and your lips with shouts of joy" (Job 8:21).

Somewhere over the next few days I found that if I just pretended she was still at the hospital, or away getting cancer research done, I could cope and the pain felt less. I think I played this mind game often. Anytime I started to feel sad, I just pretended she was at the hospital. After all, she was gone often at the hospital since she was so ill. In time, I played the game less and had to deal with her not coming home. I would pray at these times and ask God to take the sadness and let my whole family be happy again.

Diane (Carr) Farley

A Brother's Thoughts

My Sister Chris

Chris passed the day before I was born, so unfortunately, I never had the honor of meeting my big sister. I know that Chris was very anxious to see me. Even though I never got the opportunity to meet my sister Chris, I feel like she has been with me my whole life. As weird as it might sound, I feel like a part of her is in me.

One example was on my wedding day a couple of years ago. For some reason I caught myself thinking about my sister Chris. I don't know what that means and may never know, but it made me feel good that she was in my mind on that very special day. I am sad that I never got the chance to meet my sister, but I know I will get the chance.

As the years have gone by, my family has told me a lot of stories about Chris. I hear that even though she was ten years old when she passed, she had the heart and the maturity of someone three times her age. She was very strong in her faith, and that's why I am assured that I will finally meet my sister one day in heaven. I know there is only so much I can say since I never knew her, but I honestly do not believe my family would be the way we are today if it wasn't for her. I have never felt or seen so much love and compassion in my life than what my family shares for one another. On one visit I had with my family, my mother and father showed me some of the notebooks and little hobbies and toys that Chris kept during her short period with them. I did not want to show my parents how proud and honored I was when I was reading some of her notebooks. I was shocked at how much faith a ten-year-old could have in God. I felt a little embarrassed, so I kept it inside me. On my drive back home, all I could do was smile. I was happy to have read some of her favorite Scriptures and realized that we both loved a lot of those same Scriptures. Without the grace of God, I don't know how my family could have overcome the hardship that they faced. I know this because it's still hard on me, thirty-three years later. My father asked me a while ago if I would write down some thoughts and feelings about my sister Chris. I'm not writing this to impress my father, my mother, my sisters, or the rest of my family. I'm writing this to let you know the impact that this little girl had on our lives and how I believe it molded our family to be what it is today. God bless.

David Carr

Mom Remembers

Chris became our family focus, and let me say, she rose to the occasion. She had a great sense of humor and undying desire to make the best of any situation. Oh, she was a normal child in most ways and could "get" to her sisters. Chris and I spent so many hours together driving back and forth to hospitals, we actually became friends—not just mother and daughter. We would talk about everything and nothing. We would tell jokes, sing songs, and play games. Her favorite song was "Sunshine on My Shoulders," by John Denver. When that song came on the radio, she would sing right along. On our hospital trips, sometimes her sisters or a friend would come along. Some days we would make it a special day by going to the beach or museum. Most of the time during our hospital visits, a trip to the gift shop was on the agenda. Chris would wander around but eventually return to the jewelry section or stuffed animals. She purchased plenty of both in those brief years.

Chris grew in her faith very quickly. It seemed that after her pneumonia, she and Jesus had a very special relationship. She was no longer afraid of the worst tests; she would simply ask the Lord to take the pain, and He did. Chris was a friendly child who made friends with other children, patients at Children's Memorial Hospital, as well as staff members. She was often the organizer and would get other kids busy doing crafts and other activities when she had to stay at the hospital for a period of time. In a real sense those children became her small group. However, Chris did like things her way, especially at home. Chris was a "neat freak." Her collection of "stuff" was always arranged in an orderly fashion. Chris was into crafts, puzzles, reading, and writing. When Chris was able, she played outdoors, but basically she was an indoor person. She played piano and loved music. Chris had a certain energy about her and possessed a never-give-up attitude. She could be feisty, serious, and also funny and a ham.

Chris had a confident faith and peace. She was quiet but self-assured and profoundly grown up in many ways. Chris trusted Jesus her Savior no matter what! She had a strong, determined spirit and could also be stubborn at times. She had a quick temper and could stomp to her room with the best of them. But her anger never lasted very long. Chris was very special and very ordinary all at the same time.

Jan Carr

In Memory of Chris Carr

The author of the following poem never knew Chris or her family. However, Chris's story was passed on to her. As a result, God inspired her to write the following words.

This poem was prefaced with a brief note by the wife of one of the teachers at Chris's elementary school.

April 1, 1977

Dear Mr. & Mrs. Carr,

We want to tell you that our prayers are with you as you enter a new chapter in your life.

Jim has spoken several times of Chris's testimony in school and of yours as well.

Last Sunday morning before he sang a solo in the worship service in our church, he told of Chris going home and of the quiet acceptance of God's will in her life and yours. One of the young women was moved to write a poem, and on Sunday after church asked us to give it to you. It is enclosed.

Be assured that your testimony before, during Chris's memorial service, and in the years to come has had a

positive effect for Christ on those of us who love Him and
on many who don't know Him.

In His love,
Jim & Karen Vercouteren

"Little Child Lost?"

Was she strong? Oh yes, so strong!
Was she tender? They say she was.
Was she wise? Beyond her years!
And tho' I knew her not,
My soul reached out to hers;
For with her parting she left
Not sorrow but hope,
Not distress but peace,
A thirst to know the source
Of her inner strength.

Her body tho' frail
Resounds with beauty,
Because of her joy of living.
A Child—yes, and at times
Frightened, but knowing
God loved her,
She simply departed with Him.
Leaving behind only
Fond love and curiosity,
A longing for God
That only He could
Satisfy.
A child lost? No . . .
Only reclaimed
By a wise and loving

Savior.

—Sue Tillman

Her Memory Lives On

Through the passing years, Jan and I have made a concerted effort to keep the memory of Chris alive in her sisters and brother, and in our grandchildren. This chapter is dedicated to the memory of Christine Carol Carr and her unmovable love for her Lord and Savior.

Jesus Christ has truly set her free. Our personal thanks are extended to the readers of *Time After Time* for indulging us as we do so. Yes, we have many wonderful memories!

"Sunshine on My Shoulders"
Words by: John Denver
Sung by John Denver and accompanied by Chris Carr
(Some lyrics paraphrased)

The bright sun on my shoulders brings me joy.
The bright sun in my eyes fills me up in tears.
The bright sun reflecting on the water looks so beautiful.
The bright sun usually lifts me up.

If there is one day I could offer you,
That day would resemble today.
If there was one song to share with you,
That song would make you feel the joy of a sunny day.

The bright sun on my shoulders brings me joy.
The bright sun in my eyes fills me up in tears.
The bright sun reflecting on the water looks so beautiful.
The bright sun usually lifts me up.

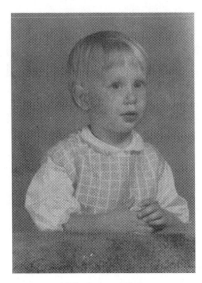

Chris at age 2

Chris 5, Connie 3, Diane 2

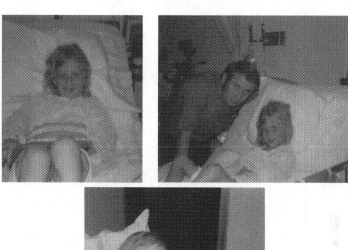

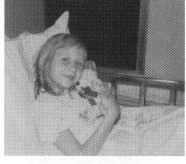

Chris in Children's Memorial Hospital having "skin grafts" on leg

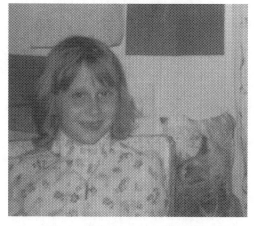

Chris at home after diagnosis

Chris 8 years

Chris in wig and bonnet after radiation in 1975 at age 8

Age 9

Chris's last birthday with us, age 10.

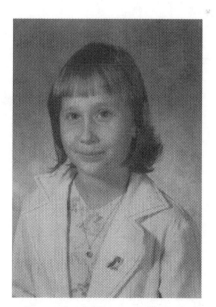

Last school picture, 5th grade

Back row: Jan, Denny
Front row: Connie, Diane, Chris
Last family picture with Chris.

David, sent from God, the day after Chris went to be with Jesus.

Jesus can overcome the darkness of your situation with the radiant and penetrating light of His revelation.

"Oh Happy Day"
Words by: Edwin Hawkins, based on 18th century hymn
(Some lyrics paraphrased)

What a wonderful glorious day
Such a wonderful glorious day
Such a fine wonderful day
When Jesus cleansed me of my sins
When Jesus cleansed me of my sins

Such a wonderful glorious day
Such a wonderful glorious day

Jesus taught me to be alert, to stand firm and pray
And to rejoice in the Lord each new day
Such a glorious day

Jesus showed me the way
Such a glorious day
Such a glorious day
Such a glorious day

CHAPTER SIXTEEN

"Oh Happy Day"

What's It All About?

Time After Time is based on Nehemiah 9:28b: "And when they cried out to You again, You heard from Heaven, and in Your compassion You delivered them, time after time." The nation of Israel paid a tremendous price for their sin and rebellion. Yet when they turned to God and sought repentance and restoration, God delivered them time after time. Friends, God does not put restrictions on how many times He will come to our aid with His love, grace, and mercy. Our faith journey is based on a true story of how God raised up and sustained a family that faced hardships and through it all experienced victory time after time. God did so through a series of dramatic, life-changing events.

Revelation

God accomplished His purposes by placing in Jan's heart the sevenfold love letter (some would call prophecy). We hear these words from the Old Testament prophet Joel: "And afterward, I will pour out My Spirit on all people. Your sons and daughters will prophesy, your old men will dream dreams, your young men will see visions. Even on My servants, both men and women, I will pour out My Spirit in those days" (Joel 2:28–29).

One in Spirit

Peter quoted Joel in Acts 2:16–21. The outpouring of the Spirit of God that Joel had predicted hundreds of years earlier occurred on Pentecost. However, the manifestations of God's Spirit did not end on the day of Pentecost. Instead it marked the beginning of the Spiritual power, wonders, signs, and blessings available to every believer in Christ and will continue into the last days. Some denominations, theologians, seminaries, and laypeople have debated these Holy Spirit happenings for centuries. As I have said previously, my intent is not to try to convince the reader one way or the other on the matter of prophecy. Rather it is to share what we experienced based on what God laid on Jan's heart seven years before all these revelations came to fruition. I simply encourage the reader to be open and not close minded, and to allow the Spirit of God to speak truth to the heart.

Recapping the Seven Wonders

Our personal relationship with Christ grew, and was stretched and challenged. Each wonder revealed to Jan was fulfilled according to God's perfect timing: 1) Chris's new birth; 2) Jan would have a baby; 3) the baby would be a boy; 4) I would choose his name given to Jan by God; 5) our finances would change; 6. my vocation would change; 7) we would have a new home. All seven events were fulfilled in seven years. How could one possibly deny God's marvelous supernatural intervention in each of these events? We did not prefabricate and make them up as we went along. We are not powerful, smart, or creative enough to do so. Praise Jesus! May He be glorified and honored forever and ever. Amen!

Dig Your Own Well

I believe God continues to use Chris's faith as a testimony and witness to others. However, it is not enough to have personally known Chris or to have heard about her faith journey. The fact is we all must "dig our own spiritual wells," so to speak. Paul said, "Consider Abraham: He believed God, and it was credited to Him as righteousness. Understand, then, that those who believe are children of Abraham" (Galatians 3:6-7).

Being Part of the Story

Every person must establish his or her own personal relationship with Jesus as Lord and Savior. It's not enough to read a book about Jesus or how one family came into a saving knowledge of Jesus Christ through tragic events. No, people reading this book must become a part of the story themselves.

The bottom line is this: we cannot receive Jesus as Lord and ride into heaven on someone else's coattails. I believe it is important for us to understand this truth. Our relationship with Jesus, responding to Him for daily guidance and salvation, is something we must all do for ourselves.

What Are You Gonna Do?

We always have choices in life. We can become bitter and hostile over our misfortunes. We can feel cheated and ask the "why" questions—why did my loved one die, why do I have this physical affliction, why am I struggling financially and in relationships, why can't I find a job, why am I stuck with a lousy boss, and so on. But friends, the good news is that we do not have to stay there. We can remove the bitter tastes that we have developed in bad situations.

Being Set Free

Please allow me to be up front and honest here: losing Chris just stinks. Anyone who has suffered the loss of a child knows exactly what I am saying. The reality of life is this. Our lives come with difficulties and at times crushing moments. However, as bad as it seems to get, the Holy Spirit can help us stay close to God's unlimited mercy and strength despite what may come our way.

Nice and Easy

Unfortunately, many followers of Christ think life should be trouble-free. Consequently they become disillusioned when the bullets start flying and they are confronted with bumps along the way. There is no question that all us of will experience problems and difficulties in life. However, as believers in Christ, we can view them as opportunities for personal spiritual growth. Someone wisely said, "You cannot prevail with God unless you have problems to prevail over." Isaiah 54:17 offers these encouraging words when trouble stalks us: "No weapon forged against you will prevail, and you will refute every tongue that accuses you. This is the heritage of the servants of the Lord, and this is their vindication from Me." Let Jesus fight your battles and nothing will prevail against you, for Jesus will give you victory!

Do You Believe This?

God can use even suffering for His glory and our benefit. Such was the story of Joseph in Genesis 37:1–50:26). The Bible tells us Joseph was the second youngest of Jacob's sons. Joseph happened to be his father Jacob's favorite son. Young Joseph did not help his relationship with his brothers because of his youthful haughtiness, arrogance, and boastful pride. As a result, Joseph was despised and hated by his older brothers. His brothers eventually sold Joseph to a bunch of Midianite merchants on their way to Egypt. As an Egyptian slave Joseph eventually emerged as a ruler over all Egypt under Pharaoh.

It's True

Through the trials of Joseph, we learn some very important and valuable lessons about the tribulations we will face in this life. It does not matter how unfair or painful our moments of suffering might be. God can and will use our unfortunate circumstances to build strong character and deeper wisdom and faith. I realize for some of you this is not exactly the answer you are looking for in your heartache and affliction. However, I would encourage you to grasp this truth. God will never waste an opportunity, regardless of how awful and negative it might be, to help us grow in Him. The secret is that we must allow Him to do so. Years later when Joseph was reconciled with his brothers, he said to them, "You intended to harm me, but God intended it for good to accomplish what is now being done, the saving of many lives" (Genesis 50:20). God can also bring good out of a bad situation in our lives if we trust Him to do so.

Our Survival Kit

An explorer or hiker should carry some kind of survival kit in case of trouble. As Christians we need to carry our spiritual survival kit wherever we go, and this includes Jesus and the truth of His Word. Our survival kit begins at the foot of the cross when we ask Jesus to heal our wounded spirits and hearts. Throughout our challenges and hardships surrounding Chris and after her death, we survived because of a persistent faith in God's grace and mercy. I believe God honors our steadfastness in all areas, including the spiritual aspects of our lives.

Building Character

There is no question in our hearts and minds that all the events we experienced with Chris, including our future ministry destination, were orchestrated by the Holy Spirit of God. In our experiences, Jesus was teaching us persistent faith. I firmly believe God helps build strong character in every Christian when the going gets tough. It is truly a glorious day when Jesus forgives and cleanses us from the sins and imperfections that He encourages us to pray about and fight each day.

Promise Never Broken

From day one of Chris's leukemia diagnosis, we put our trust in God's promises to sustain, strengthen, and guide us one day, one ask at a time. We certainly had our moments in the flesh, when we had reservations about whether God was in control of our circumstances. In our weakness, God made us stronger in Christ. *God uses our weaknesses for His purposes.* We discovered that God never reneges on a promise. Acts 13:23 says, "From this man's descendents God has brought to Israel the Savior Jesus, as He promised." Verses 38–39 say, "Therefore, my brothers, I want you to know that through Jesus the forgiveness of sins is proclaimed to you. Through Him everyone who believes is justified from everything you could not be justified from the Law of Moses."

Oh Happy Day!

First Paul was speaking to devout Jews. He reminded them about the covenant God had made with their forefathers, Abraham, Isaac, Jacob, and others. Then in verses 38–39 he was careful to say that salvation and forgiveness are for all who believe. Salvation does not come by way of strict obedience to the Law or doctrines, but from faith in Christ. Jan and I discovered this in our moments of fear. When we lifted up our guilt and doubts, confessing them in the name of Jesus, we experienced His peace and received His forgiveness. Forgiveness is only one prayer, one ask away from receiving Jesus' grace and mercy. It is a "happy day" when we realize how merciful God is, and that His covenant love will never be broken.

Chris's Legacy Lives On

Chris's life and her faith have been the driving force behind our family's life choices. Her sisters, Connie and Diane, and their families are active members in their respective churches. Chris's brother, David, and his wife are also active church attendees. We have an added bonus: our grandchildren know Jesus as Lord and Savior. It all began with Chris—her illness and eventual death. In Christ Jesus we have found a legacy of hope and unlimited grace. Someone once said, "The most depressing word in the dictionary is *hopelessness*." It is assuring and transforming to know that in Jesus we can have all we will ever need to live a life of joy, hope, and peace even in the midst of strife and heartache. Praise You, Lord, for using Chris as your instrument of truth in our lives.

Pressing On

Yes, Chris lives on in the hearts of her family. To this day, her death in some ways still pains my heart. But Christ Jesus continues to heal and wipe away my tears and replaces them with the truth and glory of His presence and salvation. Chris is with her Lord, more alive than ever. When Chris died, Satan meant it for evil, but God used her death for good and victory. The memory of Chris will live on. How God used this little girl for His glory fans the flames of our faith today.

More Than a Coincidence

No one could ever convince me that God's intervention in Chris's illness and death was just a prefabrication of some sort. Let's review the facts:

Was it a coincidence that we came to Christ in her illness?

Was it a coincidence that Chris was healed from Pneumocystics Carnii even though not one person of any age had ever survived this type of pneumonia?

Was it a coincidence that God revealed a sevenfold prophecy to Jan?

Was it a coincidence that each of these prophecies came to pass in seven years?

Was it a coincidence that the exact moment I prayed, "Lord, I want your will to be done in Chris's life," she died?

Was it a coincidence that David was born within forty-eight hours after Chris passed away?

Was it a coincidence that Jan was able to attend her daughter's funeral after giving birth?

Was it a coincidence that God called me into ministry?

Was it a coincidence that God is still using Chris for His glory?

Is it a coincidence that it took more than thirty years for God to lay it on my heart to write this book?

Is it a coincidence that there are hundreds—thousands—of galaxies in the heavens?

Was it a coincidence that God caused a forty-day flood, as recorded in Genesis?

Was it a coincidence that Joshua held up Moses' arms until their enemies were defeated?

Was it a coincidence that the Israelites marched around Jericho for seven days before the walls came tumbling down?

Was it a coincidence that God spoke to Moses through a burning bush?

Was it a coincidence that Christ appeared to Paul on the road to Damascus?

I firmly believe we cannot rationalize away God's supernatural manifestations in these events and countless others recorded in His Word. God always has worked and continues to work in the lives of His people, because He is who He says He is, and nobody and nothing on this earth can contain His sovereign will and purposes. We just need to make sure we are not hiding or running from God, because we need to run to Him.

Never Out of Touch

In those early years with Chris and beyond, we learned some very important truths. We were and are never out of reach of God's love. The same applies to all reading this book.

We are never out of reach of God's grace.

We are never out of reach of God's forgiveness (in Christ).

We are never out of reach of God's mercy.

We are never out of reach of salvation in Christ.

We are never out of reach of God's kindness.

We are never out of reach of God's righteousness.

We are never out of reach of God's faithfulness.

We are never out of reach of God's presence.

We are never out of reach of God's guidance.

We are never out of reach of God's truth (in the Bible).

My point is this. It doesn't matter how far we have fallen away from God; we are never out of reach of His reconciliation in Jesus!

Words to Hang On To

Chris's last spoken words were "Thank you, Jesus." These words are constant reminders for us that in Jesus we find strength, comfort, hope, and victory over sin and death. Pastor Randal Ross in his book *From the Cross to Eternity* sums up why we should give thanks to Jesus.

> Our generation is searching for trust and rest. We imagine ourselves in control, yet what we long for is someone, something to trust completely. We fear a chaotic world out of control. Alone and vulnerable, we become weary and crave rest even more.

> Sometimes it seems as if the world is falling in on us. We can't find a place to let go of the pressure. We cannot finish life on our own. In order to live up to life's demands and truly be all that we can be, we have to give ourselves to Someone stronger.

> From the cross, Jesus calls to us to give our burdens to the Father. His message is the same as it was throughout His life: "Come to Me, all you who labor and are heavy laden and I will give you rest. Take my yoke upon you and learn from Me, for I am gentle and lowly in heart, and you will find rest for your souls. (Matthew 11: 28,29)

The Faith Factor

Those who wish, hope, and pray solely for material rewards will one day leave this earth with nothing. However, what we take with us to the kingdom of heaven will be our faith in Christ Jesus. Friends, what we will take with us is a legacy of how we have lived our lives before God and how we have loved, treated others, and basically lived our lives. These things are far more valuable and lasting than any amount of money, power, prestige, and position we might have enjoyed on this planet. The big question that will be directed to all of us at the gates of heaven is What did you do with Jesus in your heart and life?

Good or Evil

Genesis 2 tells us God planted a garden. In the middle of the garden were two trees, the Tree of Life and the Tree of Knowledge of Good and Evil (Genesis 2:9). In verses 15-17 we read, "The Lord God took the man and put him in the Garden of Eden to work it and take care of it, And the Lord God commanded the man, you are free to eat from any tree in the garden; but you must not eat from the tree of the knowledge of good and evil, for when you eat of it you will surely die."

God gave Adam and Eve the freedom to choose. Eventually they chose to disobey God and eat from the forbidden tree. The result of their choice brought devastating, lasting effects on humanity. Sin, heartache, and death entered the world and have plagued the human condition ever since.

Choice

God gives us choices today as He did in the days of the Garden of Eden to either obey or disobey Him. If we make the right choice, we find life, purpose, promise, and hope. When Jan and I chose to follow Jesus, God provided His supernatural power, which enabled us to rise above the trials we were facing. Jesus is good all the time!

Reminiscing

Chris lived a life of conflict, trying to be a typical kid growing up while struggling with major health problems. For three years, Chris lived a life of uncertainty. Much of what she experienced in her short ten and a half years was out of her control. She was caught in a life situation much bigger than herself. In spite of it all, Chris chose not to try and solve her problems. Instead she called on Jesus to be the solution.

The Solution

The word of God offers us a solution that Chris held on to: Jesus, Jesus, Jesus, Jesus! If you have not turned to Jesus, you can do so now. When you commit to Him, He will transform your life inside and out. I truly believe that if Chris could speak for herself, she would encourage every reader to trust Jesus with his or her life. This happens when you ask Jesus to forgive your sins past, present, and future. When you make that decision, His Holy Spirit will give you a complete spiritual overhaul. *We can be assured that God's solutions will always manifest Holy Spirit conclusions.*

Let Jesus Heal You

Some of you might be haunted by the loss of a son, daughter, brother, sister, or friend. If you are being strangled by despair, discouragement, and frustration, I encourage you to lay your burdens at the feet of Jesus. There you will find healing and release from your agony and torment. I don't know why you might be suffering. I don't have the answers to the deep mysteries of life. But I do know that God has all the answers. I did not feel a sense of relief when Chris died. Rather, I felt a release when I gave her to Jesus. In the process of writing this book, God has once again drawn me closer to Him.

Where Are You?

At times we ask, "Lord, where are you and what are you doing?" When we are faced with the hardships and uncertainties of life, we often cry out in anger and frustration. God, it just isn't fair! Why don't You put an end to all evil, pain, disappointment, and death now? The Bible tells us very clearly that God will abolish the evil that began in the garden when Jesus returns to this earth in glory. When He comes again, there will be a celebration that has never been witnessed before. There will be a happy, joyous reunion of all those who have put their trust in Jesus.

The Supremacy of Christ

Billy Graham wrote in the revised edition of his book *Storm Warning*, "No wonder Scripture tells us that, at that time, 'every knee should bow, in Heaven and on earth and under the earth, and every tongue confess that Jesus Christ is Lord' (Philippians 2:10–11). If you do not receive Christ as Savior and bow to Him now as Lord of your life, the day is coming when you will bow before Him as Judge."

The Beginning and the End

Listen to John's words from Revelation 1:17–18. "When I saw Him [Jesus], I fell at His feet as though dead. Then He placed His right hand on me and said: Do not be afraid. I am the first and the last. I am the living One; I was dead, and behold I am alive forever and ever! And I hold the keys of death and Hades." Jesus is the beginning the end and everything in between.

Without Jesus, we have nothing of eternal value.

Without Jesus, we have nothing that can transform our lives.

Without Jesus we have nothing that can save or protect us from the corruption, destruction and pollution of sin.

Without Jesus, nothing can give us real peace and hope for today, tomorrow, and forever.

Without Jesus, nothing can take away the ugly sting of death.

Yes, Jesus is the living water whose well never runs dry.

Telling It Like It Is

Time After Time is a story that begins with tragic events but concludes with joy and victory, with the knowledge that there will be a better tomorrow. This book is not based on some Hollywood fairytale ending or wishful thinking. It's centered on truth. In our horrific trials we discovered the most important and profound good news of all. In Jesus we found our reason for living.

You've Gotta Love It!

The glorious truth about Chris's life and death is centered on this truth. As believers in Christ, we will one day see her again. We will not see her once-frail, perishable body but her new, perfect body, free of disease and decay. Chris is more alive than ever before because of Jesus, the "living One."

He's Waiting for You

If you do not believe that Jesus is your reason for hope and for living, if you are not sure you will spend eternity with Him, you can be sure right now. Just pray this simple prayer, and Jesus Christ will begin to transform your life, just as He has done for so many others and for me.

"Lord Jesus, I confess that I have sinned. I believe You died on the cross to forgive me of my past sins and also for my salvation. Come into my heart right now and be my Lord and Savior. I now receive You by faith. Amen."

Hallelujah! Hallelujah!

If you prayed that prayer in your heart, you are now a child of God, a member of His eternal family. This is the beginning of a wonderful journey, learning to surrender your whole being to Christ. Give praise and honor to Jesus, your new King of Kings and Lord of Lords, the One who is the beginning and the end of all existing hope, wisdom, and power. Jesus will never, ever let you down!

This life is not the end for the Christian. A joyous eternity awaits all believers in Jesus Christ. The spiritual benefits you will receive from your Lord will have an absolutely profound effect on your life. First Corinthians 15:55 says, "Where, O death, is your victory? Where, O death, is your sting?"

Chrissy's Theme

These paraphrased words of Cindi Lauper's "Time After Time," though secular, can be applied to Chris's circle of life and how Jesus was there for her and the rest of her family.

"Time After Time"
Words by Rob Hyman and Cyndi Lauper
(Some lyrics paraphrased)

While resting in bed I am listening to the sound of my
clock
With my mind on you
Hung up in a cycle of confusion is not strange to me
Looking at yesterday warm evenings nearly forgotten

A host of things remembered time and again.

There are times when you envision me moving too fast
You keep crying out to me, but I am not listening
Then you tell me to slow down,
I lag back, while the clock winds down

If you don't know where you are just look my way
And I will see you time and time again

After my photo withers and the night turns to dawn.
Gazing out of windows
You might be thinking is everything all right
Hidden thoughts taken away from the depths within,
The beating of the drum is out of rhythm.

You call me to slow down I lag behind while the clock
    winds down
Time and time again
Time and time again
Time and time again
Time and time again.

Time after Time

Jesus was close at hand with Chris and us time after time. When we fell, He was always there waiting to catch us, time after time. When the darkness of our deepest fears overwhelmed us, Jesus was there supporting, edifying, and holding us up time after time. When Chris died, the impact of her loss turned our heartache and memories of those days gone by into joy and victory; we reached out and found Jesus time after time. He would be there, ready to wrap His strong, caring, and comforting arms around us, time after time. Today this same wonderful, understanding, compassionate Savior is still teaching by correcting, training, and pulling us back when we get too far ahead of Him and He tells us to go slow. The second hand of life unwinds when we are lost in mourning, self-pity, and confusion. And behold! We look inside our hearts and find the same eternal Jesus ready to catch us, time after time.

A Storehouse of Treasures

Jesus is mentioned countless times throughout this book for a very good reason. We had a death grip on Him! There is no other way to explain it. Without His presence, guidance, strength, and power, we would have folded like a deck of cards under the relentless pressure, stress, and devastation. Without the good news of the resurrection, we would have missed the joy, hope, peace, and divine blessings that awaited us beyond Chris's grave. We never would have experienced victory in Christ. Please think about this: *what we get out of life is what we allow Jesus to put into it.*

Final Thoughts

Allow me to close our story with a poem my daughter Diane wrote. This poem is about how Diane knows at the end of the day whether she is restored in a proper relationship with the Lord.

Restoration

Restoration—what do you mean?
Are you talking about what our Lord did on the tree,
Or when He made the blind man see,
Or how He walked up Calvary?

I'm not sure you know the Word,

Which comes from above, I'm assured.
The King knows in our hearts
Why it beats, who plays what part.
He knows my desires, my deepest dreams,
To live for Him with no in-betweens.
To walk in truth, after every fall,
To cry out loud over the wall . . .
That blocks other believers from hearing Him clear,
Walking wrong ways where He's not near.

"It's a nightmare to me," I cry out,
Not because I'm perfect—but He changed my heart,
To live for Him, not myself.
Even if I have to look not smart, silly, or awful,
Doesn't matter as long as it brings glory to my Savior . . .
To own my sin and give Him praise,
My highest honor, to Him the accolades.

I fall on my knees one more time
To say, "Lord, am I restored with you?"—That's the line

Where my concern needs to be 24/7.
This is what will prepare me for heaven.
To You, oh King, I live my life.
Keep me there!

Praise Jesus! It has been thirty-five years since Chris passed away, and He is still showing up in our lives.

Time After Time!

Epilogue

Whatever God's reasons are, He chose *Time After Time* to be written years after Chris's death. Perhaps some who have read this book might question the spiritual redundancy that fills its pages. My response is simple but nonetheless true. That's just the way it was! The power of the living Christ was the only way we survived all the heartache and tragedy. I want the reader to be assured there aren't any wild exaggerations to this story.

Life is filled with peaks of joy, happiness, contentment, and fulfillment and valleys of misery, pain, confusion, and hopelessness. Sometimes the load we carry in life is more than we can handle. However, this Gospel good news reminds us God is in the midst of our ups and downs. Yes, yes! We can overcome and endure the hard knocks that can harm us along life's journey because Jesus is ultimately the One who can bear our burdens.

Time After Time continually reaffirms that Jesus can make us stronger and heal our deepest wounds if we will simply open our hearts to Him and let it happen. This is not an exercise of some mystical mind control power but a matter of Holy Spirit conviction, inspiration, and biblical revelation. Did we always get it right? Hardly! At times our faith walk was trial and error. But through all our weariness we discovered that Jesus alone could truly bear our burdens.

Jesus said in Matthew 11:28–30, "Come to Me, all you who are weary and burdened, and I will give you rest. Take My yoke upon you and learn from Me, for I am gentle and humble in heart, and you will find rest for your souls. For My yoke is easy and my burden is light."

Lay your cares and worries down at the feet of Jesus. It is a great, liberating feeling to be set free!

www.facebook.com/Pastor Denny1
Web-site: victoryandhope.com
Email: info@victoryandhope.com

Notes

Introduction

1. Romans 8:28 (NIV).
2. "Bring The Rain," words by Holly Cheney.

Chapter One

1. "Lady In Red," words by Chris De Burgh.
2. 1Peter 5:8 (NIV).
3. 1Peter 3:3-4 (NIV).
4. 1 Corinthians 2:14 (NIV).

Chapter Two

1. "It's My Party And I Will Cry If I Want To." words by Walter Gold, John Gluck Jr., and Herb Weiner
2. 1 Corinthians 2:14-15 (NIV).
3. John 16:33 (NIV).
4. Romans 12:2 (NIV).
5. Luke 8:22-25 (NIV).

Chapter Three

1. "All I Need Is A Miracle," words by Neil Christopher-Mike Rutherford.
2. Hebrews 4:1-2 (NIV).
3. Hebrews 4; 14-16 (NIV)
4. 2 Corinthians 5:17 (NIV).

Chapter Four

1. "Sweet Caroline," words by Neil Diamond.
2. Romans 10:9 (NIV).
3. Romans 10:11 NIV).
4. Romans 19:13 (NIV).
5. Hebrews 13:8 (NIV).
6. Acts 1:8 (NIV).
7. Ephesians 1:13-14 ((NIV).

8. Acts 4:12 (NIV).
9. John 14:6 (NIV).
10. 1John 1:9 (NIV).
11. "The best things happen when you're dancing," words by Irving Berlin.
12. Galatians 3:23-25 (NIV).
13. Matthew 6:31-34 (NIV).
14. "Sweet Caroline," words by Neil Diamond.

Chapter Five

1. "I Will Follow Him," words by Franck Pourcel and Paul Mauriat.
2. Hebrews 11:1-3 (NIV).
3. *"sure, certain"* (NIV).
4. Hebrews 11:6 (NIV).
5. 1Peter 1:23-25 (NIV).
6. Hebrews 12:1-4 (NIV).
7. 1Corinthians 11:1-2 (NIV).
8. 2 Corinthians 9:6-9 (NIV).
9. Luke 6:38 (NIV).

Chapter Six

1. "Day By Day," words by Stephen Schwartz (New Music).
2. John 17:15-17 (NIV).
3. Proverbs 119:105 (NIV).
4. John 16:33 (NIV).
5. James 4:10 (NIV).
6. 1 Corinthians 1:31 (NIV).
7. James 1:5-8 (NIV).
8. Habakkuk 2:4 (NIV).
9. Luke 11:11-13 (NIV).

Chapter Seven

1. "I Can See Clearly Now," words by Johnny Nash.
2. Joel 2:18-21 (NIV).
3. Lamentations 3:22-25 (NIV).
4. 2Peter 3:18 (NIV).
5. James 4:2-3 (NIV).
6. Matthew 4:23-24 (NIV).
7. Joel 2:28-29 (NIV).
8. "Blest be the tie that binds," words by Rev. John Fawcett.
9. Acts 4:32-35 (NIV).

Chapter Eight

1. "The Long And Winding Road," words by Paul McCartney.
2. 2Peter 1:3-4 (NIV).
3. 2Peter 1:5-9 (NIV).
4. 1John 4:18 (NIV).
5. Romans 6:18 (NIV).
6. 1Corinthians 12: 7-11 (NIV).
7. 1Corinthians 1:31 (NIV).
8. Philippians 3:16 (NIV).
9. Mark 9:23 (NIV).
10. "Love Letters," words by Diana Krall.
11. Jeremiah 33:3 (NIV).
12. Ecclesiastes 3:1-2 (NIV).

Chapter Nine

1. "I'll Be There," words by Berry Gordy, Bob West, Hal Davis and Willie Hutch.
2. Proverbs 3:5-6 (NIV).
3. Matthew 7:7-8 (NIV).
4. Matthew 11:28-30 (NIV).
5. John 13:34-35 (NIV).
6. John 15:13 (NIV).

Chapter 10

1. "Lean On Me," words by Bill Withers.
2. Genesis 9:8-17 NIV).
3. Mark 16:18 (NIV).
4. James 5:14-15 (NIV).
5. Genesis 49:9 (NIV).
6. Revelation 5:6a (NIV).
7. Isaiah 53:7 (NIV).
8. Luke 23:24 (NIV).
9. Bookmark, *"Lord like a filter over a camera lens. Let everything in my life be tinted by my focus on Christ."*

Chapter Eleven

1. "Just When I Needed You Most," words by Randy Vanwarmer and Tony Wilson.
2. Philippians 4:4-7 (NIV).
3. Ephesians 6:10-11 (NIV).
4. Revelation 12:10-11 (NIV).

5. Psalm 27:4 (NIV).
6. Revelation 21:5 (NIV).
7. 1 Corinthians 15:54-56 (NIV).
8. *From the Cross to Eternity*, author Pastor Randal Ross.
9. John 14:1 (NIV).
10. Timothy 4:18 (NIV).
11. "The Revelation Song," words by Jennie Riddle.

Chapter Twelve

1. "Having My Baby," words by Paul Anka.
2. Colossians 1:9-12 (NIV).
3. Luke 23:40-43 (NIV).
4. Lamentations 3:25 (NIV).
5. Proverbs 17:22 (NIV).
6. "You Light Up My Life," words by Joseph Brooks.
7. John 8:12 (NIV).
8. Isaiah 40:30-31 (NIV).

Chapter Thirteen

1. "That's What Friends Are For," words by Carol Bayer Sager and Burt Bacharach
2. Ecclesiastes 4:7-10 (NIV).
3. 1Timothy 6:18-19 (NIV).
4. Joel 2:21 (NIV).

Chapter Fourteen

1. "Brother Love's Traveling Salvation Show," words by Neil Diamond.
2. Malachi 3:10 (NIV).
3. Psalm 34:8 (NIV).
4. Ecclesiastes 3:1-5 (NIV).
5. Philippians 4:19 (NIV).
6. Lamentations 3:25 (NIV).
7. Genesis 12:1-3 (NIV).
8. Romans 10:13 (NIV).
9. John 14:6 (NIV).

Chapter Fifteen

1. "Moments To Remember," words by Robert Allen, Al Stillman.
2. John 6:35 (NIV).
3. Puzzle, *Mary And The Boy Jesus.*
4. Bookmark: *Just For Today;. Quality Industries Phil. PA.*

5. Bookmark: *What God Hath Promised*, Selected
6. Psalm 23 (Interpreted by Christine Carr).
7. Entree Titles from Christine's journal: *The Morning Bright; Tender Jesus Meek and Mild; Ah, Dearest Jesus, Holy Child; Lord Jesus, Bless The Pastor's Word; Be Near Me, Lord Jesus; Our Hands We Hold; Father, Bless Our School Today; Dear God, My Heavenly Father; Savior, Use the Gift I Lay.*
8. Doctor's Poem (author unknown) *For Chris*
9. Job 8:21 (NIV).
10. Letter to the Carr's By Jim and Karen Vercouterern.
11. Poem *Little Child Lost?* By Sue Tillman.
12. "Sunshine On My Shoulders," words by John Denver.

Chapter Sixteen

1. "Oh Happy Day," words by Edwin Hawkins, based on 18th century hymn.
2. Nehemiah 9:28b (NIV).
3. Joel 2:28-29 (NIV).
4. Galatians 3:6-7 (NIV).
5. Isaiah 54:17 (NIV).
6. Genesis 50:20 (NIV).
7. Acts 13:23; 38-39 (NIV).
8. "Oh Happy Day," words by Edwin Hawkins, based on 18th century hymn.
9. *From the Cross to Eternity*, author Randal Ross.
10. Genesis 2:9; 15-17 (NIV).
11. *Storm Warning*, by Billy Graham.
12. Philippians 2:10-11 (NIV).
13. Revelation 1:17-18 (NIV).
14. 1 Corinthians 15:56 (NIV).
15. "Time After Time," words by Rob Hyman and Cyndi Lauper.

Biblical References for the book Time After Time

New International Version-Life Application Bible
Wiersbe's Expository Outlines On The Old Testament
Wiersbe's Expository Outlines On The New Testament

Additional Resources:

Personal mementoes from Christine Carr
Personal Journals from Jan Carr
Memories shared by: Connie (Carr) Baker, David Carr, Diane (Carr) Farley, Jan Carr, Steve Carr, Beth Luther, Sandy Petrille, Carol Seidel

Poem *Restoration*, by Diane (Carr) Farley

Epilogue:

1. Matthew 11:28-30 (NIV).